REVEALED
BY DARKNESS

*To my ancestors, the elders,
who stand in the dark,
waiting for me to arrive.*

Copyright © 2021 by Chloe Elgar

All rights reserved. No part of this book may be reproduced or transmitted in any form or by any means, electronic or mechanical, including photocopying, recording, or by any information storage and retrieval system, without permission in writing from the copyright owner. This book was printed in the United States of America.

ISBN: 978-0-578-92915-6

Cover Design & Illustrations by Paulina Kisielewska, Good Intentions Studio
Interior Design by Heather Holmstrom, Studiohaha
Printed by KDP Publishing, An Amazon.com Company

Available from Amazon.com and other retail outlets.

Chloe xoxo

REVEALED BY DARKNESS

A PSYCHIC MEMOIR

CHLOE ELGAR

Mel,

Everything that you have been working towards is coming to a completion. It's time to work less and receive more. To stand tall, knowing your value and gifts. Holding that truth in your heart — knowing it it is all coming. Trust. The tides are changing.

Chloe xox

"I am not looking to escape my darkness,
I am learning to love myself there."

- RUNE LAZULI

In telling my story, my hope is that you see and feel yourself in it. We are all both soul and human beings, and we have experiences that are rooted in duality. We all know pain and fear, and it is impossible to ever compare one life path to another.

Before I begin sharing my story with you, I wanted to take a moment to recognise some of my truths. I feel responsible to bear witness to a few facts so that they do not remain unsaid: I am a white woman who grew up with certain levels of privilege. As a child, I felt this unspoken privilege and was aware of it, especially because I grew up in Malaysia. We had a maid, a driver, and our white-washed expat community clearly benefited from an unspoken racial hierarchy. As an adult, and especially during the past few years, my awareness of these privileges and the separation that they create has been heightened, especially since moving to America. These privileges do not take away from the realities of what I experienced, but they are certainly worth acknowledging. As a human, it continues to be a part of my work to evolve my consciousness and deepen my understanding of why I am here and how I can be of service. This book is one way.

Our stories are our wisdom.
Our stories are our medicine.
Somewhere along the way,
we will become aware that everything
that has happened to us,
has been for us—good, bad, dark, light.

Trust that there is a balance coming together.
Trust that the light and darkness are inseparable.
We can't have one without the other,
and it is only with both
that we can embrace our full reflection.

CONTENTS

PROLOGUE
MAGIC ARROW | 19

CHAPTER 1
ARE YOU AFRAID OF THE DARK? | 23

CHAPTER 2
REDEFINING DARKNESS | 31

CHAPTER 3
THE ELDERS | 43

CHAPTER 4
SECRETS | 55

CHAPTER 5
THE LINES BETWEEN DARK AND LIGHT | 63

CHAPTER 6
INTO THE SHADOWS | 79

CHAPTER 7
EXILED | 93

CHAPTER 8
FITTING INTO SMALL SPACES | 107

CHAPTER 9
SOLACE | 127

CHAPTER 10
IN BETWEEN WORLDS | 135

CHAPTER 11
UNSHACKLING INTUITION | 145

CHAPTER 12
THE INITIATION | 155

CHAPTER 13
THE VEIL | 163

CHAPTER 14
THE ILLUSIVE SHIELD | 175

CHAPTER 15
THE KNIGHT | 191

CHAPTER 16
EXPOSED | 211

CHAPTER 17
LIFE FORCE | 223

CHAPTER 18
INTO THE WILD | 233

CHAPTER 19
TURNING AWAY FROM TRUTH | 245

CHAPTER 20
MELDED BY THE FLAME | 257

CHAPTER 21
SEEING IN THE DARK | 269

CHAPTER 22
THE HARDEST TRUTH | 281

CHAPTER 23
BEFRIENDING DEATH | 299

EPILOGUE
FLYING ARROW | 319

ACKNOWLEDGMENTS
IT TAKES A VILLAGE | 325

A NOTE FROM THE AUTHOR | 329

MAGIC ARROW

Her cold hands shivered as she carefully wrapped the sky blue bow around the smooth ends of my hair. She playfully tussled the other side, wrangling the loose strands into another bunch to begin braiding. My tiny hands pushed down on her thighs as my legs swung back and forth, sculpting a safe and cozy seat in her lap. I breathed in, holding the icy air in my mouth as she brushed and pulled my wild, tangled hair into her kind hands, dividing it into three pieces. I loved when my Aunt braided my hair. I loved how her hands knew exactly what to do, crossing one bunch of hair over the other, over the other in a rhythmic pace. As she braided, she sang a familiar song with words I didn't know but recognised. Every word traveled from her mouth to my heart, like a string of electricity. The song felt old, as if it was sung by every woman who braided another's hair throughout time. Just as she knew how to braid my hair in that steady rhythmic pace, she knew the song too, as others perhaps had. Without effort, the song was sung and my hair was braided. It was just her and I in the room, everyone else had gone to the neighbours for (another) cup of tea and cookies. These rare moments with my Aunt Ananda were precious to me. Bramble, my Nana's dog, stayed back with us to save her prime spot at the toasty fireplace, away from the winter weather outside. Her shaggy, droopy Spaniel ears fell around her face like a cozy blanket. I liked to pretend that Bramble was my dog, and when we were visiting family in England, I followed Bramble around like her shadow, even squishing myself into her bed with her.

My aunt fastened the second braid with another bow and reached down to take a sip of her milky black tea. Bramble poked one eye open and lifted her shaggy ears up, alert to the disruptive sound of the crackling wood. From that point onward, she kept one eye partially open, as if she was aware of another presence in the room. Although I couldn't see anyone, I too could feel something new, as if the room was smaller than it actually was. I reached down to touch the bracelets Ananda always wore, decorated in colourful jewels and stones that she called crystals. Something about them sparked my interest. My Aunt wrapped me in her arms, linked them across my heart, closed her eyes, and breathed in the magic of the moment. With my braids finished, it was story time.

"What story are you ready for, Chloe?" She asked with a sense of inviting curiosity in her voice.

Grabbing onto her forearms, I responded, "Tell me something good, Aunty Ananda. Tell me a story about animals and magic."

"I know just the one," she confirmed with a strong hint of Welsh in her response. She reached her right hand to her left shoulder, touching the area where a tattoo of Kali, the Hindu goddess of death, was etched on her body.

"There once lived a magical young girl in an east land called Tibet. She was known for her tender heart and kindness as well as her courage and confidence. The elder, a healer in the village, picked her out from the group of orphans because she seemed special. She was drawn to the natural world and was said to communicate with animals. The elder began to spend time with her, sharing her wisdom and knowledge through telling her stories.

Tragically, the little girl died much earlier than they had hoped. When she died, in line with the traditions of the village, her body was laid out on a platform at the top of a mountain. This tradition was called a "Sky Burial." There on the mountaintop, her body became an offering to the vultures to eat. According to indigenous lore, the sooner the birds arrived and the more they ate off of the bones of the body, the more sacred and pure the soul was. The village saw the vultures as angels who helped transport the soul into the heavens for reincarnation, leaving the bones of the body behind. The day of the young girl's burial the vultures arrived immediately, and they ate every last bit of her flesh in minutes. Witnessing this confirmed what the elder had always felt."

CHAPTER I

ARE YOU AFRAID OF THE DARK?

"We live in the flicker."
- JOSEPH CONRAD

Twenty years after hearing the story from Aunt Ananda, I'm at the ranch and the night feels dangerous, the same way it did throughout my childhood. As the sun drifts towards the horizon, darkness slowly creeps across the field. The birds stop chirping; the horses vanish from the open fields. All I can see around me are snow-covered hills, ice-capped mountains, and icy lakes. I feel as if the night is about to swallow me whole, and tonight, I have to face it alone. The sun is still lingering on the horizon, taking a deep inhale before vanishing. I can count on my hand the number of minutes until the night's darkness sinks its teeth into me. I shudder at the thought. When night comes, everything feels uncontrollable and all encompassing—my emotions, my mind. I feel unsafe, and nothing I do or think can distract me from facing what comes with the darkness: everything I've been hiding from.

I'm here at the ranch alone by choice. Just a few months after finishing my psychic medium certification in Whistler, BC, I decided to follow the subtle breadcrumbs that led me to my family's ranch in the foothills of Alberta in the dead of winter. This haunting place has always called me back since our family bought it in the summer of 2000. It quickly became my oasis, an escape from my reality, where I could sleep in the barn with my horse every night and spend all day outside without a care.

Ever since saying "yes" to embracing my psychic gifts at the retreat in Whistler, I started feeling energies of dead beings who have passed on and no longer live in the physical world. Energies others might miss or disregard. I was always aware of a certain something at the ranch. I was always more energetically curious there, but it wasn't until I said "yes" to going there alone that my energetic suspicions turned into a knowing.

Our house, like many in Alberta, sits on stolen land that was once home to others. It was built upon the remnants of previous landowners and, before them, the indigenous people of the land. We bought the property from an eccentric, wild west businessman who called himself "The Sheriff." He also happened to have once been friends with, and fought with, Muhammad Ali. His unique idea was to create an old western town on a 500-acre lot, complete with a saloon bar in the middle of nowhere. The land where the ranch sits holds the memory and energy of death, massacre, and pain. When I return to the ranch alone, these spirits and beings come out from the shadows to speak to me. As soon as I walk through the front door and close it behind me, I feel them lining up outside, waiting for me. The empty, spacious house suddenly feels occupied and the air is thick like a sticky grey web wrapping itself around my body, keeping me up at night. Despite my terror, I feel as though I can't leave; I'm trapped in this web of energy. I'm here to learn from these energies.

As the sun continues to drift toward the horizon and the energy of the spirits grow stronger at the ranch, I recall that I've always had an infatuation with darkness. The same way that I watched horror movies as a kid, even though my mum told me not to. I couldn't sleep for weeks, if not months, after watching them, but I kept watching.

The night has always been associated with spiritual activity; "witching hour" is the term that refers to the time of night when the supernatural are at their most powerful, or when the veil between the living and the dead is at its thinnest. The term was first recorded in 1535 when the Catholic Church forbade activities during three to four in the morning because of rising concerns about witchcraft in Europe. Whether it was innate or not, for me, nighttime always felt too quiet, too still, and the air, too thick.

I remember feeling scared as a child when my parents would go out for dinner at night, and sometimes, when I was walking home alone in the dark, I would run fast and pretend a panther was chasing me. That panther was the darkness of the sky, but no matter how fast I ran he was always inescapable. I felt as though the darkness was out to get me. For me, darkness meant danger. It meant seeing things I didn't want to see, feeling things I didn't want to feel, being alone, and feeling unsafe. Since I was a child, darkness meant bedtime, which meant being and sleeping alone. It also meant monsters under the bed, strange and indescribable sensations, and the uncomfortable feeling of being alone. I was scared of falling asleep because that meant dreams and dreams meant night terrors and night terrors meant complete and utter fear. Everything stopped and became quiet at nighttime, and I was forced to sit alone with myself. The darkness was also synonymous with when, in future years, I'd cut myself and resurrect the food from earlier in the day. The darkness brought with it the parts of me who craved something insatiable, reaching out to men, food, and alcohol to feed it. It was synonymous with the shame I felt about my past and who I was. These were the meanings I gave darkness: uncontrollable, uncomfortable, and terrorizing, but there were also meanings I learned too.

When I was younger, I was cautioned by my parents not to walk alone at night in case I would be harmed when most of the city was fast asleep. There was a certain danger associated with the nighttime when everyone was asleep. In the silence of the night—the unknown of darkness—people disappeared. The darkness was dangerous, and I was taught to fear it. I took on the societal fear and assumptions about darkness that people gave me, and despite my parents' warning, there I was at the ranch, in the middle of winter walking along the dark country road—alone.

Tonight, nightfall at the ranch is still like that panther from my childhood. It is bloodthirsty and irreverent. It chases and taunts my mind, and I know that if I stop running, it will grab me by the ankles and force me to surrender to myself. My perception of darkness determines its impact on me. The more scared I am, the more energy and collateral my fear mind has to work with. I don't even know why I am scared of it; I just am. My fear overrides any and all happy thoughts like an unconquerable computer virus. I was scared of what and who I felt and couldn't see in the dark. The slightly uninvited and incredibly outspoken presence at the ranch caught me off guard. These women who I had never met in life, and had only heard stories about, were suddenly there with me in my bedroom, in the dark, in the middle of the wild.

I used to read the ancient story of Inanna, the Sumerian Queen of Heaven. She was a queen who craved the underworld, the darkness. Before she left to journey to the underworld below, she dressed herself in a festive crown and beads to mark the special occasion. When she entered the underworld, she was forced to shed parts of herself—first the crown and then the beads. As Inanna descended into the darkness, she was forced to discard her material possessions, showing they were actually worthless and didn't provide any safety.

The depths of the underworld unraveled the parts of Inanna she once thought were important to her identity. The darkness of the night and the arrival of my ancestors has the same effect on me. It dismantles every part of me that has me believe I know myself. The silence and stillness of the night lets me peer into myself and be present with my true essence, not the essence clouded by my possessions or my ego. There is a sharpness about the silence and stillness of darkness that forces us to strip.

When we go to bed, we wipe clean our faces and remove our masks, undressing to our most vulnerable selves. We prepare to send our conscious minds to sleep and enter a different reality, the subconscious realm. This is a time when everything else is hidden—our fears, worries, and unexpressed desires. Whatever it is that we don't show in the waking, light-filled world, exists in the darkness, in the times we sleep. This is a space where we are forced to be with the truth.

I had to journey through this darkness to be able to know who I am today. But before I left on that journey, I had to promise myself to light a torch of self-forgiveness and kindness, and I had to constantly remind myself that every part of my journey—both the dark and light—was important in unraveling and discovering who I am. Discovering is a constant journey, and we must stand with both fear and love, dark and light, in order to fully embody our power. We cannot exist without one. This is my story about rediscovering and accepting my darkness. This is my story of becoming whole.

What happens to you when you are in darkness?

What does the "dark" mean to you?

What are the "dark" parts of you?

How do you respond to them?

Do you allow others to witness your darkness?

Do you honour the dark?

CHAPTER 2

REDEFINING DARKNESS

"Intuition is seeing with the soul."
- DEAN KOONTZ

I sleep lightly when I'm at the ranch, especially in the winter months. The sun's arrival excites me, boosting me out of bed and into my snug thermals. One hand searches for my thick mustard beanie as the other signals my dog, Ollie, to follow me upstairs. The pitter-patter of his tiny paws on the hardwood floor creates droplets of joy in my heart. As I push the front door open, the crispy cold air explodes over my face, shocking me into awareness. I carefully step down the slippery steps, carving fresh footprints into the new snow. We're alone in the early hours of the day, and the silence of our surroundings overpowers any small noise. I can hear the horses in the distance, standing together to create warmth. The sun is only beginning to rise, creating a stunning tapestry of pastels in the sky. Towards the barn, I hear one of the barn cats scratching on the sliding door. My eyes focus on Excalibur, the lead gelding, the protector, who instantly looks up in alert, noticing something far in the distance. A coyote, the trickster, lurking through the snow from one treeline to the next. Excalibur is alert to the threat, but not alarmed or in danger. I quickly called Ollie to me, who was minding his own business playing in the snowbank not far away. Despite his valiant personality, Ollie would be no match to a hungry lone coyote hunting at dawn. The trickster plants himself at the top of the treeline, hidden by the hill's towering shadow. Watching the coyote's every step, Excalibur begins trotting towards the fence on the opposite side of the pasture away from the trees, followed by his loyal herd of mares. Their movement extinguishes any advantage the coyote might've had. Once again, they are all safe.

Perhaps we all have a place in the world that magnifies our magic; a place where all of our senses are heightened and we notice every twitch and tick. Every land holds magic and every ancestral land has a magical history in its roots. Magic is something we are all born with. It is a natural part of our world. It is a connection to life outside of the physical, an appreciation and belief in the energetic realms. Magic and intuition are interchangeable. If we believe in magic and work with it, we are connecting to our intuition. When we work with and use our intuition, we are experiencing magic. We are all intuitive and therefore magical, and we have within us the ability to sense and perceive energy. It's not as obvious to some as it is to others, but we all have the capacity. Whether it's a random knowing to take a different route home, someone's name popping into our heads right before they call, or seeing an energetic projection like a colour, orb, or silhouette in front of us. I like to use my intuition to choose my clothes every morning and what colour mug I'll drink out of. We all sense energy in various ways and some places in the world seem to make everything louder and more noticeable.

There are locations on the planet that have been identified as "spiritual hotspots" or vortexes, where the energetic presence is magnified: Sedona, Bali, Maui, Stonehenge in England, the Pyramids in Egypt, Mount Shasta in California, and Ayers Rock in Australia. These are spots that have been seen as sacred sites historically and people have gone on pilgrimages to visit them. Perhaps these are places our souls know deeply, a place we have lived before, holding the memories and stories of our past selves. You can't stay sleeping in these places, and you can't hide. These are the places that wake us up and force us forward. I often hear people say that places like this either welcome you with open arms or spit you out, depicting energetic alignment or dissonance. Nature and the ranch have this effect on me. The uninterrupted silence, the thick blanket of stark darkness, the sudden spatial awareness of myself and what's around me. I always knew the ranch was this place for me, but it wasn't until I was there on my own that it was confirmed. It's no surprise that our family ranch sits on one of these global energetic vortexes, located next to Banff, Alberta.

During the daylight, these energies that I sense aren't scary. They leave me curious and open. At night, in the dark, I'm terrified. Not only does the idea of a coyote in the dark scare me, but the fact that I can't see it makes it unbearable. The darkness amplifies everything, including our sensory experience. When it's dark, we tend to be more aware of what is around us, because we can't see. When one of our senses is abandoned, the other senses become heightened as if to compensate for the loss. When we lose a sense, we lose a form of control. When we can't see, our fear mind becomes active, and when we feel fear without awareness, it tends to take over.

Even though I know theoretically that spirits are present in the daylight, I feel safe and more at ease when it is light out. It is comforting to know that people are awake, and if I need to find someone to interact with, I can. I can look outside the window and see what is going on around me. I can message my mentor and know that she will reply within an hour. I can call my husband Faris and he will pick up. I can go for a walk with Ollie to see the horses and feel safe. I can read my book or watch a movie and not feel intensely aware of the echo created by the silence. I can sit in silence meditating without worrying about what I will open my eyes to. I can distract myself with relative ease.

The second night alone at the ranch is one of the longest nights of my life. No matter how hard I try to take a deep breath, the evening air only makes it to the top of my throat. My dog, Ollie, sits beside me rubbing his soft and silky coat against my wintery pale calf. I grab his rubber apricot frisbee and launch it towards the vacant saloon ahead of me—another empty building. No one is around us.

We are alone in the middle of the dense hill country of the Albertan Rockies and now the horses are asleep. It feels as though I have accidentally locked myself in a haunted house, and I can't find my way out. My mind flickers to years ago when I watched a documentary. It was about two men who climbed the Andes during winter. One of the friends got left behind with a broken leg, and each morning was a question of whether the next day would bring snow and blizzards, or sunshine. Every night he would anticipate all of the dangers that came with darkness—hungry animals, below freezing temperatures, many unseen and unknown threats to his life. Every morning his eyes opened, he questioned whether he would make it to see the next sunrise. Settling into my bed at the ranch tonight, the same sensation fills me. It feels like a frantic mix of looking forward to the morning and fearing the hours of darkness.

This isn't the first time I felt the presence of spirits around me, but it is the first time that I consciously am aware of them and my connection to them as an adult. I know that by acknowledging my gifts and saying "yes," I have subconsciously invited them in. My psychic light that apparently said "OFFICE HOURS OPEN" is on without me knowing it, and it is the only visible light for miles of darkness. They know I am here.

In the foothills in the thick of winter, it begins to get dark at 5 p.m., and the sun doesn't rise again until around 8 a.m.—fifteen hours of darkness. I climb up the soft, carpeted staircase towards my mum's bedroom, the lightest place in the house. Instead of anxiously waiting for the unknown, I decide to take control of my fear and set the stage for a peaceful evening.

The cold limestone tiles of my mum's bathroom sting my feet as I reach over her freestanding, porcelain tub touching the icy, stainless steel handle. As the heat of the water and candlelight fill the room, I begin to feel a subtle sensation of warmth and peace. I climb into the bath, wine glass in hand and Ollie sitting by the door as if he's standing guard. For a few moments, my fear of the impending night disappears, and I feel a sense of connection and joy for being here. I feel a twinge of magic

> "Nothing in life is to be feared,
> it is only to be understood.
> Now is the time to understand more,
> so that we may fear less."
> - MARIE CURIE

for this life as I listen to the healing sound of Trevor Hall's voice sing his song about not rushing healing. The flickering candlelight dances on the walls, creating shadows with its flame. All is well.

Suddenly, my happy silence is punctured by the alarming sound of something hitting the floor downstairs. My heart jumps into my mouth as I fly out of the bath and onto the frigid bathroom floor. I look at Ollie, wishing for a moment that he is a large scary wolf that can protect me instead of a friendly miniature Australian shepherd. I grab my mum's winter robe, take a large inhale, and walk downstairs to investigate the source of the noise. Nothing looks out of the ordinary on the main floor, so I take another large inhale and creep down the gloomy staircase into the basement. I drag my left hand on the wall, searching for the light switch. Once I turn on all of the lights, I begin to look around, moving from room to room searching for something I fear finding. I leave the basement bathroom to last. There is always something about the mirror in the bathroom down there that doesn't sit well for me. There sitting on the cold limestone floor is a picture frame, face down. As I pick it up, a string of shivers shoot up my back. I feel as though I'm not the only one standing in that small bathroom; the pressure of someone's hands are on my shoulders.

The photo is one of my mother's grandmother and her family. A black and white photo, which I had seen the night before in my mind's eye while I was asleep, but I had never seen this photo before then. I never knew that it was hanging on the basement bathroom wall either. But for some reason, I suddenly feel like I know, without a thread of a doubt, that my ancestors and any other spirits who inhabit the land are all there with me in the house, watching me. Even though I'm completely terrified, I try my best to swallow my fear and make it seem as though I'm unfazed. My mind tells me that they know and that spirits know the truth; I can't hide from them, they can hear my thoughts. I open my mouth to declare in the most nonchalant voice I can muster, "What a beautiful photo, right Ollie? I'll put it in the boiler room for now, so it doesn't fall again." I emerge from the basement with Ollie at my ankles only to realise that while I was downstairs, the sun completed its nightly descent into darkness. My time to set the stage for peace and calm is up. As I recalibrate to the energy upstairs, where the air feels lighter, I realise that another noise is coming from my mum's bedroom. This time, I run. The bathroom sink tap is running, and I know that I certainly didn't turn it on. This time, I have a harder time pretending that I'm okay. I turn the knob, close my eyes, and ask for it to stop. I resist opening my eyes, imagining what I might see in the mirror when I open them. I remember learning that mirrors are spiritual portals, ways to see and communicate to spirits and also travel to other realms. I'm scared and I don't feel safe. My fear is activated and it feels impossible to shift it in the dark. It feels like my ancestors are there to torment me, rather than to talk to me. I can't deny their presence, but I also don't want it like this. This will be one of the longest nights of my life. I finally fall asleep at 6 a.m. — Netflix blasting the new movie of the moment—until the promise of light's arrival feels close enough, and with it, a sense of safety. Even when I did fall asleep for a moment in the night, I was immediately woken up by something. I was sweating; I saw something in the darkness. I felt something on top of me; I noticed a strange noise. The combination of my fear and what was actually happening wouldn't allow me to settle.

Even though I can just leave the ranch after that night, I decide to stay for those two weeks. Something inside of me keeps me there, regardless of the sleepless couple of nights I had. I feel as though I'm going through an initiation with my ancestors and with darkness itself. They are the ones who invited me to come to the ranch in the first place. So it is time for me to face my fears of spirits and work through the blocks that

I had built up around connecting with them. As a child, part of what strengthened my fears was a feeling of being alone.

As I lean back in my bed at the end of another day and pull the blankets to my chin, I peer into the dark shadows of the house. Those dark corners of the ranch house are left up to my mind's interpretation, and my mind reflects my pain and demons back to me. The dark corners remind me of times when I wrestled with my self-worth. They remind me of the consecutive days and nights when I would sit alone on my red couch, eating nothing but five green grapes and biting the tips of my fingers until they bled. They remind me of times I felt utterly alone. They remind me of a time when I wasn't here, a time when I couldn't feel anything, a time when I didn't know who I was. Like the panther from my childhood, these dark corners are inescapable because they exist within me, and I'm afraid they will be resurrected in the night. But day by day, I start to find comfort in my ancestor's presence.

It was during those two weeks at the ranch when my experience with darkness started to change, and I began to see things differently. So much of my life I had felt alone. I felt misunderstood, unsupported, and unworthy. I always felt like I was the rock for many, but there wasn't much holding me up.

Throughout those moments of solitude at the ranch, there were some key characters who nudged me forward. I call them "the elders," guardians sprinkled throughout my life to guide and protect me and to remind me of my truth in spirit and physical form.

Something that is missing from our modern-day, global culture is an intimate connection with those older and wiser than us. Those who can help guide us. An intimate connection to our past loved ones is also absent from our lives today. Looking back, I now wonder if what I was most scared of was the intimacy and love my elders offered me in the darkness, rather than the darkness itself.

Do you prefer daytime or nighttime?

When it's dark, do you feel more afraid than you are in the light?

What is it about the dark that scares you?

Were you afraid of the dark as a child?

Do you have any memories from childhood about what happened in the night?

CHAPTER 3

THE ELDERS

"Someone I loved once gave me a box full of darkness.
It took me years to understand that this too, was a gift."
— MARY OLIVER

Since I was a young girl, I was in search of elders—women who could teach me about who I am, where I came from, and why I'm here on this planet. When the student is ready, the teacher will appear, and so, for me, they did. For me, elders are both living and dead, waiting for us in the silence and showing up whether we notice them or not. They are our guides, our soul family, our ancestors, and the souls that contracted to be with us in this lifetime. They show up to invite us into a space that penetrates the story about who we think we are. They point to a path of truth and purpose. Our elders know us beyond this lifetime and this personality, and they help us remember our roots.

The ranch wasn't the first time I felt my ancestors show up. They had shown up in my life before many times, but it was always more of a whisper. The year that I went to the ranch was the year that I had really decided to work as an intuitive and take the leap professionally. Once I had made that decision, it sent a signal to my ancestors that I was ready for more. Before that year, they had been working with me behind the scenes, keeping their presence and messages relatively unfelt and unseen, allowing me to straddle the fence of believing and not believing. That year at that ranch, the volume was increasing and their voices were dialed up. I couldn't ignore them, or my intuition, anymore.

I felt them grow louder when my husband Faris and I were traveling in Asia after we got married right before I went to the ranch. The idea of spending two weeks at my family ranch, alone, in the thick of winter, dropped into my mind as we were speeding down the bumpy, Bali-village road on our rented scooter. The bright sun was ferociously burning the back of my neck as I gripped tightly onto Faris's sides, taking in the scene of abundant rice paddy fields and friendly, mud-brown water buffalo. My ancestors were also the ones who pushed me to go to Bali.

Months before, in the early fall, I was on the coast of Vancouver with my psychic friend and business partner at the time. We were checking out houses for our upcoming psychic medium retreat, and we had just exited the car, talking about places to travel to, and walked into a metaphysical store. Just as I mentioned Bali, a woman with a head of untamed fiery red curls walked out of the store and blurted out, "You should go to Bali this winter," without looking at me or saying anything else. We were both pretty stunned, but this also wasn't a situation that was out of the ordinary for us, especially when we were together. It was a big deal for Faris and I to go to Bali for a month in December during the holidays and disappoint my family, but after that synchronicity, we had to.

It was a capricious thought, daydreaming of Albertan winters and deep layers of snow while I was soaking in a tropical paradise, but the spontaneous thought felt familiar and non-negotiable. It was an intense, immediate knowing, rather than a wandering thought, something that I have since come to recognise as intuitive guidance. It was my ancestors, the elders, guiding me. It was time for me to deepen my connection with them and my intuition.

A few years after the ranch and after moving through several initiations with darkness, I met an elder who really pushed me towards growth, and she invited me to confront a new depth of darkness. She was a rather large, Viking-like woman named Ingrid Kincaid—the rune woman. Her name, like her energy, was a blend of Scandinavian, ancient European, and wintery Scottish roots. Her hair was wild like that of a cave woman and white as snow. Despite her size and blood relations, she had a calmness about her that felt grandmotherly. She spoke in an unexpected feminine softness that would sometimes trick me into believing she didn't hold energetic daggers in her hands. I never knew when she was going to puncture my stories and reach the deepest available truth. Her relationship with the runes felt familiar. To her, the runes were not tools or symbols; they were divine beings, just as we were. Her psychic ways were unassuming, and her unwavering search for truth was led by a deep partnership with questions. She had a steady passion and respect for questions and how when we embrace them, rather than fear them, we open space for so much magic and truth. She always said, "Nothing I say is true. Everything I say is true. The truth lives in the questions." She wasn't about proving her gifts or showing them off, but when she needed to guide you back to truth, she would, irreverently.

I had chosen to spend the weekend in Sedona with Ingrid, nine other witches, and one man (whom we referred to as our token wizard). Together, we dove into the realm of the runes, giants and the mythological Nornir. These ancient symbol signatures represent divine Nordic beings. They are oftentimes referred to as divination tools and used to connect to the spirit realm. Ingrid called herself the "Rune Woman," and over that weekend she introduced us to new, ancient truths about the runes. Ingrid led us through a path of darkness, and her mission was simple: to invite us into the darkness of our ancestry and remind us who we are in our wholeness. She dressed in black, which contrasted perfectly with her wild, white curls. She wore skulls and carried bones and furs from Nordic animals that were sacred parts of her rituals. She reminded us that at some point in our ancestry, we were exiled from our home and that a common tragedy of the western world is the lack of connection with our ancestry and their stories. She fiercely represents the North, a place that knows darkness like no other. A place that lives in darkness for many months of the year, and as such, has a deep and meaningful relationship with it. She wanted us to sleep, eat, and breathe darkness, and her goal was to gradually purge the fear and conditioning that told us darkness was bad. By denying the dark and hiding from our own darkness, we had left behind ancient, magical parts of ourselves. Throughout the weekend, she had us chant "dark" in unison several times.

On the first day, we sounded like people whispering in a movie theatre. We were afraid of saying the word dark and the potential punishment that might accompany it. We wanted to run and hide from it, but a week later, we were yelling "dark" at the top of our lungs.

In western culture, humans call for light so aggressively, and it is everywhere. We are obsessed with it. We pray for sunshine. We chase the sun. We say "love and light" in an attempt to associate the two. Throughout our world, everything is spoken through the lens of light: sunrise, sunset, summer solstice, winter solstice. In Nordic traditions, the day begins at midnight, and it is known that darkness always precedes light. In New Age spirituality, we focus on ascension and transmuting into higher states of consciousness, which are deeply rooted in the light. Whether consciously or subconsciously, there is a hierarchy which depicts the dark as less than.

Ingrid taught us that in the Nordic traditions, the dark is honoured. The dark is valued and respected just as much as the light. When the sun sets, it is common practice in Northern Europe to turn to the east, where the dark rises. Instead of seeing it as "sunset," they see it as "nightrise." Night is rising, and the sun is disappearing into the darkness. Each nightrise is a time to celebrate how the dark returns to us, rather than simply mourning the loss of the sun. To leave the lights off and sit in the darkness, welcoming all that it brings with it. The light and dark, together, represent our entire existence. One alone cannot show the whole picture.

Ingrid felt like the mystical grandmother that I never had. Her fierce and unconditional relationship with the dark gave me the permission to explore my own. Her poignant words planted seeds into my life, inviting me to explore my own understanding of the dark and my ancestry with a new lens. Her authentic expression summoned me into my own. Her sense of intuitive power sparked my own. Her deep and ancient connection to her ancestors led me to explore my own. Sitting with her, I felt as though she already knew me, without judgment or barriers, and so I was able to fully be myself and bring all parts of myself forward. Her presence invoked a deeper healing within me. She revealed a new level of the deepest truth: you can't know yourself if you are hiding from yourself.

The weekend workshop started with an initiation ceremony. Ingrid asked each of us to bring a staff without any explanation or description of why or what we would be using it for. Leaving certain details out left us in the dark, giving our minds free range to create all sorts of stories about what might or might not happen. She invited our fear into the circle. The first night, we each had to stand in front of the room with our mysterious staff, and claim our place in the circle. Easier said than done. The moment my fingers wrapped around the raw, smooth wood, an electric current shot through my body, as if it was lighting it on fire and gluing my white ribbed turtleneck to me. At random, people began to saunter to the front of the class holding their intricately decorated staffs. My mind jumped between preparing what I would say, analysing the path forward so I wouldn't trip and fall, and looking for the fastest exit from the room. Logically, it didn't seem like such a big deal; I had plenty of experience speaking in front of groups. Energetically, I felt as though I was being asked to walk through an indescribable portal, which I could never return from. This portal was going to clear out any previous fears, beliefs, and stories I had about darkness that kept me from its magic.

We continued to learn that honoring darkness doesn't end with the Northern Europeans. For ancient Egyptians, darkness means the beginning, the empty expanse of nothing that precedes human existence. For the Chinese, darkness manifests in the yin and yang, showing how duality can be both competing and complementary. Sometimes it is merely a dot of darkness in a space of light. At other times, it is a dot of light in a space of darkness. Without darkness, we don't know the impact of light; opposites give each other meaning. Without the dark, we stop growing.

While living in Malaysia, I witnessed another type of celebration of darkness. January 28th marks the beginning of the three-day-long Thaipusam Festival in honour of the Hindu God Lord Subramanian on the full moon. It was a celebration where Hindu men and women gathered to pilgrim from the oldest Hindu temple in Kuala Lumpur to a religious site at Batu Caves. They journeyed while carrying various offerings—up to 100 kilos in weight—on their backs and covering their bodies in piercings.

What intrigued me the most was the way their bodies were pierced. Piercing might not even be the right word to describe how they sacrificed their bodies. Worshipers impaled their naked torsos with long metal skewers after entering a ceremonial trancelike state. The piercings were called kavadis, meaning suffering, and nothing of the impaled bodies was hidden from onlookers' eyes. Those who were impaled marched without fear of judgment, asking Lord Murugan for strength to overcome the obstacles they faced, both externally and within themselves.

The colours, smiles, and cheers of the onlookers couldn't cover up the struggle in the impaled people's eyes as they walked up the 272 steps to the cave temples. On this day, this day of celebration, people carried their suffering and sacrifice so that everyone could see it, and that hit me hard. Years after watching this procession and celebration, I realised darkness was never out to get me. My darkness and struggles reveal me. They are an integral part of me, and a part to be celebrated.

Ingrid made it apparent that our suffering, our darkness, isn't meant to be hidden or stuffed down our throats. Stay with the questions, the unknown, the parts of yourself you are afraid to show. Don't make assumptions about those parts. Our suffering is a celebration of who we are and who we are becoming. My suffering is meant to be seen, to be adorned like a festive, celebratory piercing—not hidden. To leave out my suffering from my story is like erasing a part of myself, a part that has allowed me to plant my feet firmly and confidently on the ground today. And yet, I've always felt pressured to hide my dark parts, to not talk about them, and consequently, I've been ashamed of my darkness—the nights I binged myself until all that was left was bones. The nights I drank too much or saw too many men. These parts are a part of me as much as the parts that I am open to sharing. They are my contrast.

It wasn't until I began connecting with the elders and Ingrid that I was able to truly see this. They gave me permission to see these parts of myself differently. They shared their stories, which allowed me to find myself in them and their journeys. They sat with me in my darkest moments without turning away or anxiously trying to fix or solve me. They held the space of the dark and the light without wavering. They were supportive the same way that a tree offers sturdiness as I lean up against it. They introduced me to a different type of love. They introduced me to myself.

Ingrid was the first teacher who invited me to question the concept of light. She asked questions that I didn't think about. She saw the world from the eyes of the ancient ones, the giants who were here before the gods—a time before we saw the dark as evil or bad and the light as good and pure. She calls herself a dark worker, rather than a lightworker. In her eyes, our world is out of balance and we are losing the dark, not the light. There is too much light. You can't sleep in a city in pure darkness, anymore. Lights are everywhere: outside, in the sky, on our phones, oven clocks, and smoke detectors. Even out at the ranch, where we are supposedly in the country, there are nights where I could see the lights of the city projected onto the dark hills of the wild as if the light was slowly marching into the dark. We can't escape the light. Life is not always love and light, and Ingrid had us explore why we project it onto everything. What are we hiding from? That weekend in Sedona, we stopped ourselves from incessantly smiling and trying to be "all light" and instead, we sat with what had been forgotten and pushed aside. Every time I meet with Ingrid, she takes me back into a place of witnessing the abandoned magic of the dark.

Do you ever feel a presence around you when you're in the dark?

Have you ever sat in the darkness with your ancestors
and the people who have walked before you?

Do you know who your ancestors are?

Do you welcome them or do you turn them away, when they come knocking?

What happens to you when you feel a presence around you,
do you feel love or fear?

Who are 'they,' the elders, for you?

What elders do you have in your life?

CHAPTER 4

SECRETS

"Nature never deceives us; it is always we who deceive ourselves."
- JEAN-JACQUES ROUSSEAU

I was born with the energy of secrets. I couldn't completely grasp what they were and why I felt them. Every family has their secrets. Poisonous secrets that birth distance and barriers. I felt the secrets in my family. They were hiding in the unfriendly looks I witnessed between my mum and my Grandpa, and the awkward sensations that I felt between my dad and his sister. I felt it in the static energy at extended family gatherings in the summer. The air held unspoken rules of what to not say or ask. The destructive counterpart of secrets were revealed in the fiery arguments that became a scheduled part of the day between my parents.

Just as we were taught to tie our shoelaces before leaving the house and to brush our teeth every morning and night, we were taught to keep secrets from one another. When I found the picture of my maternal ancestors lying on the bathroom floor at the ranch, I felt those secrets again. The picture was of my great-grandmother, her two sisters, and their mother and father. It was in their eyes and the way they stood together, placing their hands on one another's shoulders like distant relatives or strangers would. Their expressions were emotionless but they said everything. Fear was dancing behind their perfectly composed expression. The photo was a storyteller, and as I looked into their eyes, I heard their voices. I felt deep sadness and pain in my heart. I felt shame.

The origin of the word, "secret" is the Latin word "secretus," which means to separate or set apart. When we hold a secret within ourselves, we create a barrier between two hearts, two points of connection. The thing about secrets is that they never remain as that. They penetrate through everything the same way water is able to cross the impermeable blood brain barrier. They don't stay put. They travel, and they grow, mutating into bigger and more treacherous forces.

Secrets are a way to control others, to keep someone in the dark of their own life. They create an illusion of protection. Secrets are energy, just like thoughts. They don't dissolve over time. They stay locked away, until they are released. The energy of secrets does not die with their masters. It continues on, passing through the blood barrier into the lineage and the next generation in the family, up the roots of the family tree like a venom. My whole life had been filled with secrets, some I knew and some I felt. Even as I write this, I feel trapped and unable to share one of these secrets with you. Are these even my secrets to tell? And if I can't release them, what do I do with them? And what does it mean when you are good at keeping secrets? What do we do with the secrets that have been passed down to us?

The secrets that I felt in my family, on both sides, ran deeper than my parents' generation. These were secrets about pain, death, abuse, adultery, jealousy, abandonment, betrayal, heartbreak, and power. They lived deep in the DNA strands of our family, woven together and knotted by each new generation. Every ounce of shame, pain, and mess was wound up tight, disguised by a perfect knot. It felt like the heaviness that each family member held was too much to be with. Rather than speaking about it or sharing it with others, these secrets were shoved into the darkness in hopes that they would simply disappear.

There was a part of me that knew that I couldn't carry on with this generational job. The weight was too heavy. I wasn't willing to live my life, carrying around a bundle of old, thick, rotten rope.

What do secrets mean to you?

What secrets do you feel and hold inside of you?

Does your family have secrets?

How do secrets impact you?

Are you good at keeping secrets?

Is shame hidden behind the illusion of perfection and control within your family?

"The obliterated place is equal parts destruction and creation.
The obliterated place is pitch black and bright light.
It is water and parched earth. It is mud and it is manna.
The real work [...] is making a home there."
- CHERYL STRAYED

CHAPTER 5

THE LINES BETWEEN DARK AND LIGHT

"The snake that crawls among the roots would not lose its venom."
- MALAYSIAN PROVERB

I'm scared.
I'm scared of failing.
I'm scared of it all.
I'm scared of dying.
I'm scared of losing love.
I'm scared of losing me.
I'm scared.

I didn't always understand darkness as being love. To fully grow into this understanding, first I had to understand how I started defining light and goodness. The brain is quite passive, and the majority of our learning happens in our younger years. We learn things unconsciously through observing the world around us and the people in it. My first definitions were given to me when I was little, they weren't mine. They were someone else's. They were given to me within fleeting moments of my childhood, and those moments gave structure to my blank, unbiased mind. The paint I later dumped onto my life's canvas was forced to fit within those lines and definitions—the lines others created, the fears and beliefs they had. I was enslaved to my environment.

I suppose a third-culture kid is the right label for me. For a large chunk of my life, and still sometimes today, I feel rather otherworldly and different than others. I've always been deeply sensitive and emotional and oftentimes felt like I was living in a different reality to the rest of the world. It doesn't feel like a mistake that my mum jokingly used to say that I was an alien. As Debra Silverman said in an astrology reading I did with her, I don't fit in anywhere. When we visit our family in England, we are seen as the foreigners who never lived there. In Canada, I am known as the Canadian with the British family, and in Malaysia, I was always an expat.

All of my family members, relatives, and ancestors are British. My mum grew up in Windsor and we all like to joke that she is related to the royal family. Interestingly, our last name spells regal if you play scrabble with the letters. My dad spent most of his childhood living in Wales. As the story goes, he's always been a bit of a womanizer, and somehow picked my mum up at a gym bar one night. Not much later, my brother was born and 17 months later, I arrived. Just before my birth, my dad moved us to Calgary, Canada, where our Canadian adventure began. Just before I turned five, he moved us again, this time to Kuala Lumpur, Malaysia. As people usually pieced together pretty quickly based on where we've lived, he worked in the Oil and Gas industry. My brother and I started school in Kuala Lumpur and began living a very different life from our British relatives. The world became our oyster, and we traveled all over, making various tropical paradises our new home. We lived a privileged lifestyle, but our lives also proved the point that money doesn't buy happiness.

When I was 12, my dad started working more and more in Dubai, and he unofficially moved there soon after. My mum decided for us to stay in Malaysia. At the time, I didn't process it this way, but looking back, it was clear that my parents were not really together anymore. From then on, their relationship would begin to make less and less sense, and anything they did do together was more for show or to keep the illusion going. What we didn't know, but all assumed in one way or another when my dad moved to Dubai, was that he also secretly embedded himself in a new relationship, creating a new family and life away from us.

Growing up in Malaysia had a huge impact on my brother and I; every summer we would return to England and Canada, and we felt like outsiders. We didn't understand their lives, and they didn't understand ours. Instead of sharing stories with our extended family members about our scholastic accolades and achievements, we would usually return to England in the summers with outlandish stories like our drivers son being tragically eaten by a python, and members of our school community being tied up and robbed. Instead of waiting by the phone for the school to announce a snow day, we waited by the phone to find out who called in the bomb threat. Rather than bringing me mice to the front door, our cats would bring us dead snakes. There were too many degrees of separation, and a short summer visit was barely enough to create a substantial connection. From then on, we would always feel distant from our family. In 2000, my mum decided that we needed a more solid place to come back to in Canada, as opposed to a hotel room at the Best Western complete with maple syrup lathered pancake stacks every morning, and so we bought a townhome on a luxury ranch property in the foothills. I looked forward to summers there more than anything so that I could be with my horse Mac and my horse club friends, and feel connected to my Canadian roots where I felt most at home. But my life on the ranch made me feel less and less at home in Malaysia.

Constantly feeling out of place and not at home coupled with feeling emotionally out of control, I was always looking for sources of safety, acceptance and approval, and I turned to others to find that. I remember sitting on my mum's Monet-inspired quilt in her perfectly imperfect eclectic room in our Victorian apartment in Malaysia; I watched as she picked apart every inch of her body in disgust staring at what, to me, was her beautiful reflection in the mirror. I remember wondering why she hated herself so much. I never understood what she was talking about, as she held onto her bony hips and thighs in complete repulsion. I remember feeling terrified that she may rip skin off of her delicate body. I sat there on her bed as she tore through her closet desperately looking for her worth. This moment will remain etched into my mind for an

"When women lose themselves, the world loses its way.
We do not need more selfless women. What we need right now is more women who have detoxed themselves so completely from the world's expectations that they are full of nothing but themselves.
What we need are women who are full of themselves.
A woman who is full of herself knows and trusts herself enough to say and do what must be done. She lets the rest burn."

- GLENNON DOYLE

eternity. From her, I learned that being "good" and "acceptable" meant looking a certain way. I also learned that my body probably wasn't a safe place, or somewhere I could feel at home in.

Lily, my friend from high school, embodied an unattainable level of "good." Her hair always looked like it was freshly permed into chocolate brown ringlets, which bounced like yo-yo balls as she moved. Her voice was a blend of Mariah Carey and Whitney Houston: a mix of jazz and pop, while being angelic. She played piano and guitar with an ease that I'd expect from John Mayer. Her body resembled the musculature of Britney Spears circa the "I'm A Slave 4 U" music video. She was amazing at sports, even though she said that she "didn't care for them." She held an unmistakable attitude of not giving a shit and acted as if she didn't care and didn't try. Despite bad grades, teachers loved her and sought after her and all of the boys wanted her. And I believed it. I believed that she was just one of those people who was naturally good at everything. She was seemingly perfect with a complementary rebellious nature. I wanted both: perfection and rebellion. I don't even remember when it happened, but somewhere along the way, she became my best friend, as if by befriending her I would become her. Again, another definition of "good," how I was supposed to be in this world, was ingrained into me.

In elementary school, most people referred to me as a doll. I was really cute, small, and "perfect." At that point of my life, perfect and small were one and the same. I had big, symmetrical, ocean-blue eyes, porcelain white skin, bright blonde hair, and mysteriously dark, bushy eyebrows. Everyone gave me a lot of attention for my looks. They commended me on my beauty. At that age, I translated that to mean my beauty and looks made me "good," reinforcing what I learned from my mum in her room years ago as she picked her body apart.

I was pretty round during those "awkward" early teen years. It was an unpleasant time. In Asia, it's very common and acceptable to comment on people's appearances, especially their weight. Apparently weight is a sign of prosperity, because if you are chubby you obviously have enough money to indulge in sweets. It's more or less celebrated. I felt really fat, ugly, and unlovable and focused on staying hidden as much as possible. It didn't help that my brother was tall and handsome and stood out like a shiny trophy. While I was celebrated for being fat, he was commonly referred to as a "young Brad Pitt" by strangers. If I hadn't seen a family friend for some time, they would greet me saying, "Wow, Chloe, you've gained weight!" While this was happening, I was also feeling everything. I felt my feelings, my family's feelings, and the feelings of people around me. I felt like a swollen balloon, ready to pop.

Growing up in Malaysia, one of my favourite people was our maid, Lanie. She started working for our family when I was seven, and she stayed until I went to high school. Lanie was like an older sister. We told each other everything, and we played and cooked together. She brushed my hair; we went to Mariah Carey concerts together, and I felt safe with her. I always hated when she had to leave to go home at the end of the week.

I would sit on the stiff and ugly quilt of her twin bed, watching as she packed up her day bag and changed her clothes. I always wondered why she had to get ready for her husband to pick her up. Wasn't she just going home with him, to their home? She would change out of her raggedy, hand-me-down clothing and put on a feminine, flowy, and showy outfit. She always wore heels, something I found strange. I loved her height without the clunky heels. As I watched her dress up for what seemed like a first date with her long-time husband, a pang of sadness would rush through my body. I never quite understood what the sadness was. I knew I'd see her again on Monday, and I knew that she was going home. But I didn't know where home was, or what home was like for her. She knew everything about my home, and I knew nothing about hers. I asked her questions about her makeup and why she was applying it. I asked the same way an investigative journalist would poke and prod someone until they got the truth.

Her perfume smelled like artificial roses and candy, the type that brings on a headache. The makeup she used wouldn't hide the bumps and craters in her skin, and as she worked to cover it, I felt my pang of sadness tighten. She worked hard to conceal the parts of herself that I loved in order to package herself up for her husband. Her laughter was loud and contagious, though it had a similar artificial aspect like the perfume. I didn't quite believe the perfume or the laugh.

I walked with Lanie down to the guardhouse where we met Callie, our hefty calico cat who loved taking naps on the pavement. Lanie danced down the steep hill in her thick platform heels, day bag in one hand and my hand in the other. Her sweaty palms spoke to mine. They relayed to me a subtle anxiety. The sun was setting, and soon the bats would emerge for their nightly dance in the sky. I watched the bats fly around our garden, swooping down as if they were painting the sky with strokes of darkness. We sat together on the black iron love seat that lived on the steps of the Victorian-style guard house. Still holding hands, I felt her heartbeat quicken. The sound of a choking exhaust pipe disturbed the stillness of sunset. We could see a silhouette of a motorbike climbing its way up the long, steep hill to our apartment complex. He was here. Her husband had arrived.

Lanie hopped off the seat as if it were on fire and wrapped her arms around my body in a motherly, loving embrace. I could smell her sadness cutting through the candy perfume as she yelled to me, "Bye, Clo. See you on Monday." She swung her tiny leg over the back of the bike, and the same arms that were wrapped around me moments ago now enveloped her husband's body. Her fingertips grabbed the bottom of his jacket. He didn't stop or get off the bike to greet me or her. His helmet barely hid his face. His eyes were dark; his body was swollen. He was no prince charming and, to me, he felt more like her father than her husband. Lanie once told me that she married him so that she could stay in Malaysia, and get a better job, so that she could support her family back home in the Philippines. She married an older Malaysian man so that she could fulfill her duty to her family, as a daughter. When she told me this, I knew that she never loved him or enjoyed being around him. She was doing her job. He passed Lanie a plastic bag filled with an orange milky tea, tied together with a rubber band. She took it, barely brushing his hand. It felt cold, transactional, and impersonal. Her eyes held a great sadness in them, but she was being feminine and subservient to her husband. She was following some unspoken rules, dancing like a beautiful puppet. She was being "good."

When I was in high school, my mum had a subscription to the GUESS monthly editorials. I would spend hours memorizing the images of the gap-toothed models in her magazines, wishing that I could switch places and bodies with them. Their lives seemed so perfect, and they were so sultry and beautiful. Mum had everything, every style of jeans—button fly, lace up, zip up, low rise, extra low rise, snake skin in all colours, leather. I knew her waist size range and compared it to mine as I tried on every pair. You name it, she had it. I learned that it was having the body, the clothes, the money, and the man that made a woman a woman.

Growing up, I learned that darkness is best hidden behind beauty. I remember watching the fairy tales where the witch conceals herself in the image of a beautiful princess, and it wasn't until she was safely in her power that she revealed her dark and ugly self to the world. Every morning I witnessed my mum cover up her dark birthmark, which sat across her left eye with strategically placed and unreasonably expensive makeup. Hardly anyone knew about her birthmark, and sometimes I felt like even she forgot about it, until late at night and early in the morning when she was with herself in private, looking into the mirror.

Many psychics and mediums have told my mum that the birthmark is a sign of a branding from a past life. She was branded for being a witch; she was marked for being different. Whenever I watched her cover it up, I felt a hot stabbing sensation in my abdomen; I could feel her disgust for it and I could hear her harsh thoughts telling her she was ugly. I always felt confused when I heard her speak about herself negatively, because I always thought she was very beautiful.

Living in Malaysia, I was also painfully aware of a certain bias in the beauty industry. Asian women always made a fuss about how "beautiful" I was and how white my skin was. Make up stores were filled with shades of white foundation, and billboards were plastered with Caucasian models or Asian models with unnaturally white skin. As if white women and white skin was more attractive or desirable than darker skin colours. I always wondered why.

We are taught that women must be beautiful, easy on the eyes, and princess-like in their appeal. This is something that was enforced and then reinforced in my world over and over again. I always wanted to be small. I wanted to feel small and look small. I never liked wearing heels because they made me look bigger and taller. They made me stand out when I wanted to hide.

My perception of what made a woman "good" was defined when I was young and those definitions ran deep into my belief system. They controlled me, subconsciously. I knew I needed to look a certain way, be agreeable, and have men like me (which equated to not giving them trouble). I fit between the lines, and I had become domesticated. Though my leash and collar were invisible—like the societal beliefs pushed onto me—I quietly wondered what it would take for me to be wild and free. To be more than just good and light, but also embrace the other sides of me, the darkness.

The ideal woman was introduced to me pretty early in life, and I was subconsciously taking notes as I listened to men of all ages comment with their judgment on women's presence and behaviour. Surprisingly, one of the men in my life who had the biggest impact on this was my brother and his friends. He was pretty vocal about the kind of woman he desired and supported. In school, he liked the confident and unique girls, but the common denominator was that they were all petite. In his mind, the ideal woman has freshly baked goods always available, a well-stocked kitchen with many delicious and accessible snacks, and a professionally designed home, and she is always ready to have people over. He created such a strong avatar of this, because of what we grew up around. I noticed that my mum never seemed to meet his expectations, which he voiced frequently. She rarely baked and if she did it was usually a boxed Betty Crocker cake. She was oftentimes in an ugly mood and hardly ever had guests over.

I always remember when we would go and visit our cousins in the summertime in England; my brother would praise our aunt, who was the embodiment of the ideal. She always presented us with a warm, well-designed home with lots of delicious food ready for him to eat and many, many things to do in and around the house. Whenever we left her house, he would always say things like, "I wish I lived there" or "Their life is so much better than ours." I took notes. I had to hide and purge any quality that resembled my mum, the darkness. By the time I was in high school, I would bake and cook my brother and his friends goodies on demand. I made it my tool of exchange. Whenever I wanted something from him, like his car, I would quickly whip up brownies, a chocolate cake, or homemade chicken pies from scratch, even if it was 3 a.m. I loved receiving praise from men for being who they wanted me to be. For a short moment, it made me feel like I was enough. I loved feeling their adoration for me. Though only temporarily, it dissolved my fears of inadequacy and abandonment. I felt wanted.

That's the thing about expectations. When we mold ourselves to fit others approval, we hide. We are all born as unique beings and we grow up learning that the way to survive and thrive in our society, is to fit into a narrative or prototype. Where is the invisible line that sits in between what we truly desire and what we do to survive? So much of what we do is ingrained in us to keep us alive. Strategies and beliefs that have been bred into us from generations and generations of pain and repression. Women haven't exactly had the freedom to claim their power and true happiness. We all carry within us a memory, or a collection of memories of abuse, death, persecution, repression, and oppression. Whether it was our soul or the souls of our family members in our lineage, it is in there, and as we walk along the path of awareness and growth, we peel back the layers and pull the threads of trauma that keep us from claiming our sovereignty. The irony is that the only real threat to my survival in my childhood was me.

Do you lean toward being a good girl, or a bad girl?

How did you learn the meanings of good and bad, and how do you see them now?

Are there parts of you that you keep hidden?

What types of women have you been surrounded by?

How do you see yourself?

Who were your role models growing up and what did they teach you?

What were you praised and rewarded for as a kid?

How do you define beauty?

Some days
I am more wolf
than woman
and I am still learning
how to stop apologising
for my wild.
- NIKITA GILL

CHAPTER 6

INTO THE SHADOWS

"We all begin as a bundle of bones lost somewhere in a desert, a dismantled skeleton that lies under the sand. It is our work to recover the parts. It is a painstaking process best done when the shadows are just right, for it takes much looking."

- CLARISSA PINKOLA ESTÉS

The wild, white wolves of the Arctic north are some of the only animals on our planet that have been virtually "untouched" by humanity—free and wild. The closest village is 1,000 miles from their territories, and human contact is unknown to them. They aren't scared of us, and their behaviours haven't yet been influenced by us, like their wolf cousins in Yellowstone Park. Their trust hasn't been betrayed by man.

These beautiful, snowy white wolves are part of a lineage of wolves that goes back 10,000 years. They patrol the land and live this very dire, challenging life as a predator. Every time they eat, they must risk their lives. For every seven hunts, they may only make one kill. And as the summer months dwindle, the pressure to eat grows. Soon, there will only be winter darkness, and they will face the long nights. If ill-prepared, they will face them hungry.

As winter approaches, the 12-week-old pups—who only know summer's light—meet darkness for the first time and may never make it through the harsh, long winter. Not all of the pups will survive its harsh test. Darkness is the true test of survival for every living soul.

Like the pups, I played with my darkness and walked the line between dark and light more than once. I quickly learned which parts of myself (and my darkness) I needed to hide and which parts I didn't in order to fit in. I did it all secretly. I managed to keep everything in line and have everyone believe that I was the perfect, pretty, straight A's young girl I needed to be to be "good." I fit within the lines that created my understanding of what was good. But, behind closed doors, I was a cheater, an alcoholic, a smoker, a cutter, a klepto, and a liar. I became aware of my mysterious ability to lie and get away with it at a young age, and I had an uncanny ability of being able to talk my way out of most things and hide everything that I wanted to keep hidden. I won everyone over with my smile and my eyes.

I realised my ability to get away with things came from my ability to feel what others were feeling and, oftentimes, hear what they were thinking. I quickly realised that this was something that my brother didn't seem to be able to do well. He always got caught. Watching people being able to hear thoughts in the movies, I knew there was some truth to what I was doing. There was a part of me that felt curious, intrigued, and excited. I could do it too. I could hear other people's thoughts. I could speak to animals. I could feel other people's feelings. This became a powerful asset, because it meant that I rarely got into trouble. I learned that this was a way that I could make sure others liked me.

I started driving illegally in middle school. I drove my dad's golden Volvo and most of the time, I was drunk or drinking. He was rarely in Malaysia, so his car was always available. I managed to never get pulled over by the cops, which I attest to my intuition. I would get a sudden flash of hot fear flooding through my body, and I would change my course or pull over and imagine that my car was invisible, in response.

I would be the person who the people in my life wanted to be. I would show them what they wanted to see and have them feel what they wanted to feel. I masked my darkness by becoming a chameleon. I've always played the part. Whatever or whoever you need me to be, I'll be. Having the skill to be who people wanted me to be, I lost who I wanted to be.

I hid my true self because I feared that if I showed exactly who I was, I would no longer be safe or loved. In psychotherapy, this is how the shadow self is created, which was first introduced by Carl Jung. We learn to hide away the parts of ourselves that we fear are unlovable, unworthy, and unacceptable. The shadow holds all of our repressed desires, emotions, and impulses, keeping them hidden from our conscious awareness. From the moment we are born the shadow self is created, becoming a powerful force of arguably unnecessary protection,

"The painful things seemed like knots on a beautiful necklace, necessary for keeping the beads in place."

- ANITA DIAMANT

creating the false belief that we are safe as long as we keep these parts of ourselves hidden.

Our shadow houses what society deems as unacceptable qualities and behaviors. Whenever we witness someone we love being rejected for a part of themselves, that piece of ourselves then gets put away into our shadow. For example, if someone else was reprimanded in class for talking out, we are then taught indirectly that speaking out is a part of our shadow self and we begin to bury that part of ourselves away. For women, we are taught from a young age that we must be pretty, thin, easygoing, fun, good home keepers, pure, stable, have it all together, and confident (plus all of the other conflicting messages we are fed through the media). Anything that falls in between these lines is stowed away, hidden from plain sight.

In my family, I quickly learned that thin, controlled, and pretty women were treated with more love and adoration than moody, emotionally expressive, "unstable" women. Most of the time my mum was the opposite of the ideal, and it was clear that she wasn't loved for it. My dad hated these powerful parts of her, as did other men. I'll never forget one summer when we were back in England, and my mum was fighting with my grandpa. He was so angry at her, and he yelled, "You are such a rotten woman with a horrid temper." I don't remember why he was upset with her, but it wasn't uncommon for him to say critical things about her under his breath, and he certainly praised and noticed my brother over me, no matter my efforts for his attention.

Throughout my childhood, my mum's weight changed incessantly. She went up and down on the scale so much that I always expected the scale to crash. And as much as her waist line fluctuated, her mood followed suit. The mood in our home reflected the tropical weather in Kuala Lumpur. You always knew that a torrential thunderstorm was coming. You braced for it.

In 7th grade, a friend of mine came over during one of these downpours. The moment it began, she politely told me that she didn't feel comfortable staying, called her mum, and left as soon as she arrived. Her response to my homelife shocked me, because I was used to it. My brother and I had become well acquainted to the massive outbursts of emotion and uncontrollable moments of rage and sadness.

I remember being at the beach in Malaysia, watching my mum walk in her swimsuit, and feeling my dad's disgust with her. I remember feeling his response to her appearance in the pit of my stomach: it felt full of judgment. This wasn't the first time I felt someone else's emotions in my own body, but the strength of his reaction stayed with me. I remember feeling an immediate knowing that I couldn't let myself look like that, cellulite and all. I remember deciding that I never wanted a man to have a response like that towards me as I walked away. I never wanted a man to cringe at my backside. I decided that if they were going to judge me, it would be because they desired me and not because they were disgusted by me. I wondered what he was really disgusted with. Was it her appearance, or something to do with who she was? Something about my mum rubbed my dad the wrong way. She was a witch. She showed her shadow self. And he hated it. Subconsciously, I decided that I would control what I could, which was my looks, my body, and the way I acted. I trained my mind to see myself and my body the way that I felt men would.

My dad was rarely pleased with my mum. He stopped bringing her to business dinners early on once she demonstrated a lack of agreeableness. My mum was known to ask challenging questions, and to go places in conversations that people were taught not to. She wasn't afraid to raise her voice, cry, or engage in heated discussions, even if it was in front of my father's client or during a business meeting. Instead of veering away from those types of questions that others do, she leaned into them. The irony is that these dinners weren't always exactly formal or stiff. They were oftentimes accompanied by bottles and bottles of wine, or jugs of beer, and ended with my dad passing out. It wasn't unusual for my brother and I to be woken up in the middle of the night, hearing my parents yelling at each other. My dad would be returning home from the bar, or a night out with his friends, completely inebriated and slightly obnoxious. I remember sometimes his friends would be dragging him in the front door like a lifeless corpse, whilst my mum yelled at him. I always wished that I could help, or ask my dad why he did that. I was sad for my mum, her heart always felt heavy and punctured. I wondered if she ever actually slept. I don't know when it exactly happened, but my dad stopped sleeping in their bedroom when I was still pretty young. Mum claimed it was because of his loud snoring, but I knew it was bigger than that.

My dad's favourite topics stayed on the surface; my mum could only go deep. She was also known to complain at restaurants and cause quite a stir with management at hotels, which my dad loathed. When my mum wasn't around, my dad and his friends would swap unfriendly stories about their wives and belittle them to no end, while eyeing other female customers and the scantily clad servers that they called the "Heineken girls." I'm sure they all believed these women were there for their entertainment. I would sit and listen, trying my best to fit into the box of what I thought they wanted.

When I was 13, I started bingeing and purging to erase my reality, to fit in the lines of what I learned was expected of a woman, to be a certain size. I'd heard of bingeing in movies; I'd read about it in books. Girls secretly talked about their weight and ways to stay skinny in the locker rooms, and I was drawn to it. It was a way to reverse the past—to play god. I could eat what I wanted, or do what I wanted, and then erase it. I had complete control; it was my way to live how I wanted but still

> "If people are denied certain parts of relationships
> they need as children,
> they hunt for these parts as adults."
> - LISA TADDEO, THREE WOMEN

> "In the middle of the journey of our life
> I found myself within a dark wood
> where the straight way was lost"
> — DANTE ALIGHIERI

fit into what men wanted or what others expected of me. Puke it up, release it from my body, and remove it from my memory.

Bingeing was the perfect way to distract my attention from the pain I was feeling at home and in my body. I had started to gain weight in middle school, a reflection of the emotional weight I was carrying. During that same time I desired to be loved and seen, especially by men. I was beginning to feel unworthy of them and ugly. I was at a time in my life—adolescence—when everything began to feel like too much; my eating disorder presented itself as my way through. It offered me some form of control as I ventured deeper into the dark and unknown world of human adolescence.

At the same time, I also started to cut myself, burn my hands with lighters and cigarettes, and hit myself. Sometimes, I would get so upset with myself that I would try to hit my head as hard as I could against a cement wall. I even would try to throw myself onto the gravel floor or against tree bark so hard that I'd injure myself. I would get so upset with myself for being the way I was. I couldn't accept myself.

I was also always angry and never felt like I had someone to talk to. Upstairs, my mum was angry, yelling at my dad or just speaking and swearing to herself. Downstairs, my brother was angry. He would lock himself in his room and blast Korn, Slipknot, Rob Zombie, and Marilyn Manson at full volume. I could hear thumping on the ground, and I just knew that he was thrashing around in his room. And in my room, I was angry. Most of the time, I didn't even know why I was angry. It didn't always feel like my anger, and I hated the feeling. Dad was always simpler than my mum, less moody and more fun. He didn't activate me like my mum did. Time with Dad always meant surface conversations, drinking, restaurants, and simple socialising. At the time, my dad was still my hero and my mum was the woman from his narrative, crazy and unstable. At the time, Dad was easier to love than Mum was.

Later that year, I managed to disappear even more by convincing my parents to rent the apartment beside ours and knock down the walls so that I could have my own space, alone. As the years went on, we continued to rent more apartments and make more holes to create more space for the chaotic energy that lived amongst us, even though my family would fit well in one apartment. I found the demolition symbolic of the hole-filled lives we were living. We had it all, but like a donut, something in the middle was missing. And yet the destruction of the walls continued, and I got my own apartment where I was able to put up emotional walls and easily hide my darkness.

Again, I was alone, despite my desperate cries for help. This would be the space where my depression deepened. This would be the space where I would binge and purge until my body could no longer stand. This would be the place where I would stay up all night running on the treadmill that I asked my mum to buy me, running toward a wall, in a dark room in the back of the apartment, alone. No one was around to reach out for support. Alone in a foreign country with Dad in Dubai and mum lost in confusion and fear of what was happening to her daughter. It was his first year at university, and my first year without him physically around since birth, and his absence made a big difference. No one could shake me out of something like Sam could. He was my best friend. I was alone and awake in the dark of the night. The night, my time to myself, was when I would soak in my pain. It was when I would twist a knife in my skin for a type of sick pleasure. I had an addiction to the depths of my darkness and the pain that came with it, but I showed no one.

Who are you in the shadows when no one is around?

What are some parts of your past, who you have been, that you feel shame or judgment about?

What about yourself do you hide from others?

If you were asked to be vulnerable, what would you share with the world?

What stories keep you trapped in your pain?

What are some qualities about others that really rub you the wrong way?

Can you see a mirror reflection into yourself?

What have you buried away from your awareness?

CHAPTER 7

EXILED

"Loneliness is a sign you are in desperate need of yourself."
- RUPI KAUR

Living alone meant that I could get away with eating nothing and have it go unnoticed. I could hide my darkness. The only foods that I allowed in my apartment and in my body were green grapes, Diet Coke, and the occasional homemade fruit salad, which I would pour pulpy carton orange juice over. You see, liquid made bingeing that much easier. Purging these items was simple: I barely had to touch my mouth with my pointer finger before it all returned to where it entered. It was pretty painless. The problem was that when it comes to bulimia, it's not always about a pain-free experience. Sometimes, the pain is the point. Like cutting, it allows me to focus on an external pain, so that I can forget about the emotional pain that consumed me and swallowed me whole. I was trying to forget my pain. I was rejecting my dark emotions, and they manifested as self-harm. My way to control it was to stuff down my darkness.

As night came again and the rest of the world was asleep, my eternal darkness came alive. That's when my hunger for pain grew, and I would find myself in my back kitchen rushing to make as much food as possible. The kitchen countertop displayed my internal chaos with the mismatched food scattered across its top. These mismatched dishes would soon be my source of relief. Grilled cheeses oozing with melted butter and burnt edges, three packets of Maggie noodles in MSG-filled chicken seasoning, a pho-sized bowl of sugary cereal and milk, baked Belgian waffles stolen from my mum's kitchen lathered in maple syrup and butter, three slices of bread with peanut butter and jelly, and a large glass of water to wash it all down. In one breath, I ate everything in sight with no thoughts of what was to come next. I chugged the glass of water as if I were chugging against the largest and fastest Oktoberfest beer drinker, barely taking a break to breathe. Suddenly, fear would overwhelm my body like a rash. Fat. My body immediately swelled up, and I felt the waistband of my cobalt blue gym shorts dig into my sides. I wished they would cut into my flesh and let my fat pour out, as if I were performing liposuction on myself. I filled my large, pint-size glass with more water and ran to my bathroom to perform my daily ritual of purging. This time it wouldn't be so easy, as if my body's defense against purging increased with the amount of times that I did it in a day. This was going to take some effort. This was going to hurt. I stuck all three trembling fingers into my mouth and down my throat, as if I was reaching to pull my stomach out. As the water rushed out of my mouth, still holding my fingers in the depths of my throat, my legs began to shake. I dropped to my knees, hoping that I would still be able to create enough of an arc to entice the food to come up. I always thought that it was easier to do this while standing, but today, my legs wouldn't hold me. The instant rise and drop in blood sugar that my body was used to at this point caused a systemic shutdown. I stayed here, continuing to scarf down water and push my fingers deeper into my throat until I finally began to purge something. My greatest fear was now possible: that some food would stay where it was and my body would expand in size—fat, ugly, disgusting, shameful. I took a break from punishing myself to look in the mirror. My eyes were crimson and my skin was translucent.

I made my way over to the large red couch in the living room and reached for a DVD to distract my mind from the impending fear of fat. Marilyn Monroe appeared on the screen, and I spent hours with her, alone in my apartment. As I watched her in pain, I saw myself. Every time I watched the story of her death, I wished that we could switch places. That I could be as beautiful and adored as her. Or that people would care as much about my own desire to disappear as they did about hers. My dad didn't even notice me, and my mum seemed too scared to do anything.

I obsessively questioned Marilyn's reasons to die, while also feeling a shameful desire to intimately know why she chose death. She had everything, I thought, as I sat in my beautiful apartment in one of the wealthiest neighbourhoods of Kuala Lumpur. And so did I. I had a life that many kids dreamt about with more space, food, and money than needed. I had parents who gave me so much freedom that their knowledge about me could be likened to a cave dweller's knowledge of world events. I had a driver, a maid, and my own apartment, and I was desperately alone. All I could feel was my mum's loneliness, my dad's absence, and my resulting lack of grounding.

I chewed my fingers, bit by bit, cuticle upon cuticle, until I felt something. Biting as hard as I could to rip the skin away until my hands started to shake and drops of red blood glittered on the surface of my thigh. I gnawed until each finger bled and throbbed uncontrollably. I grabbed a tissue, compressing the swollen area and pushing down hard so I could feel my heartbeat. I was completely numb in my thoughts, lifeless and relieved. I grabbed one of the many boxes of plasters in my graffiti-covered desk drawer and taped each trembling finger, again, pushing to feel the life within me. Looking up, I saw the words "love" and "beautiful" scratched out with deep grooves on my previously white IKEA desk and replaced with cigarette burns and melted wax. Each finger pulsating aggressively. I finally found my breath. These were the fingers that caused me pain; these were the fingers that brought me relief, love, and joy. I stood up dizzy and began my daily practice of cleaning up the evidence. Collecting each Band-Aid wrapper and crimson red tissue and throwing them into the bin already filled with the shameful after-effects of my bingeing and purging.

Each day followed a similar sequence, only differing by what I stuffed into my mouth within a matter of minutes and how much I was able to purge out. Every morning, I felt embarrassed as my Filipino maid

Nori would come to collect my garbage, dirty clothes, and bring my room back to a scene of perfection and normalcy. Pulling my blinds up to allow streams of burning-bright Malaysian sunlight to clear the forbidden darkness of my destructive space, exposing the ivory white bars that were placed over our windows for security.

I had been out of school for several weeks now, and it was the new normal. No one really knew what had happened to me, though I'm sure they all assumed the worst. Everyone witnessed my monthly disappearance, both in body and spirit. All of my friends had disappeared; no one came to visit anymore. It was just me, alone, smoking cigarettes, drinking Diet Coke, and obsessively eating only five green grapes a day. I wasn't there. I couldn't feel anything and I certainly didn't know who I was.

The night before my IB exams, I was hiding in the bathroom crying on the floor in the dark. I couldn't hold the pressure that I felt around me. These were some of the worst months, and my mum was in her own darkness, lost in how to help me, feeling her daughter slipping away. She knocked on the door, and I yelled back in anger for her to leave me alone. I felt past the point of help. She knocked again, this time mentioning with a desperate tremble in her voice that Mrs. Rahim, my teacher, was on the phone for me. The moment her name left my mum's lips, I felt warmth move through my body. Why was she calling? She had never called before, nor had any of my teachers, especially this late. The alarm and unexpectedness of her name woke a small part of me up. My mum insisted that she wanted to talk to me. I pushed myself up from the floor, opened the door and grabbed the phone. "Chloe, hi sweetheart. Look, I know you're not feeling well and it all feels too much. Here's the thing, you are going to your exam tomorrow. You know more than most of the students in the class, and I will not let you miss this exam. You are going. I'll be there the whole time. You just need to get yourself to school. I am here and I will be there." Instead of arguing or shutting down, I just listened. There was something in her voice that felt different. I believed her. For the first time in months, I didn't feel alone. I felt seen and understood by Mrs. Rahim. She didn't mention my weight-loss or lack of school attendance. She didn't follow my fear tactics and stay away from me. That night, instead of giving me space, she entered my space and gave me what I needed, strong and unwavering unconditional love.

My parents rarely knew how to help me or how to manage my darkness. My Mum was too close to it to see it. When I was 13, my parents bought me a horse in Canada. They rarely said no to me when it came to things that I wanted, partly because they didn't know what else to do. His name was Mac, and he was also 13. Despite his thoroughbred breeding and blood relations to the best racer from Kentucky, we got him for almost nothing because he was about to be sold to a meat factory. Although we didn't get the full story, it seemed like he had been sold because he was difficult to ride and was pretty anxious. He didn't fit in the box of a perfect race horse. He was discarded for his darkness. The day he arrived on the ranch, no one wanted to ride him because of his intense speed and hot-headedness. The moment I saw him, I felt as though I knew him, the pain in his eyes and the warmth of his energy. He was deeply sensitive. You could tell that Mac felt everything on an extreme level, even for a horse. Like me, his sensitivity volume was dialed all the way up. I hopped onto his back and felt the power of his heart and strength between my legs. We both felt everything, and it made life challenging for us. No one wanted to ride Mac and whenever we went on group rides, they would always comment on how wild he seemed. Whenever we returned home, Mac would hop and skip down the hill, like racehorses do. It didn't always feel great on my body, but I was never bored. The truth is, I was his source of safety too. I never judged Mac or told him that he was too much. I loved him for it. The thought of getting another easier horse never crossed my mind.

One summer when I was 15, we were all getting ready to go on a big afternoon trail ride. Everyone was already outside the barn sweating in the sunshine, tightening their cinches and swapping jokes. On this day for some reason, Mac wasn't having it. No matter how many times I tried to, he wouldn't let me put his bridle on him. The thing is, I was just over five feet, and Mac towered over me at 17.5 hands. No matter how calm I was, if he pulled his head up out of my hands to avoid the bit, I couldn't do much about it. Our head wrangler stopped by the stall to see what the delay was. She asked me to step aside, and marched her bowlegged self around the left side of Mac. Melinda was a great teacher, but she had a temper. She always had a cigarette nearby, and we often theorised that her coffee was spiked. I felt her pain, and I always tried to be nice to her. I felt like she had a hard life, and that she was used to people being hard on her. I felt like she too was sensitive, but she never had anyone support her in it. She never had a teacher call her up the night before her exams to love her. She felt lonely. Her untamed frizzy blonde curls never quite fit in her scrunchies, and you always knew when she was near from the sharp sound that her boots made on the floor. She was fiery. Patience wasn't a virtue of Melinda's, nor Mac's. She squished beside him, nudging him in his hip to shift over. She grabbed the leather bridle from my hands. I had a feeling Mac wasn't going to obey, but I was happy to pass the job over. The moment she touched the top of his head with her right hand, he swung his head up into the sky, smacking Melinda on the face. Her right hand rebounded from the shock and furiously whacked him across the face. I had never seen someone hit a horse before and witnessing it created rage inside of me. I desperately wanted to shove her aside, even though a small part of me felt empathy for the pain that I knew she was feeling. She managed to force the bit into Mac's mouth, despite their clear conflict; she walked away silently. We never spoke of it, and I never asked Melinda for her help with Mac again. I needed to protect him from people who didn't understand him.

I spent every hour that I could with Mac in the summers at the ranch. We swam, slept, and ate together. No one could beat us in a race, and when I was with him, I felt stronger. When I was on his back, I felt safer. Summers would always go by too fast; the end of August would arrive, and we would leave to go back to Malaysia for the school year. Leaving Mac created an intolerable pain. I spent the first few weeks back in Malaysia in a dark depression, writing letters to my friends in Calgary pleading for them to send me updated pictures and stories of Mac.

Back in Malaysia, alone, I was no longer safe with myself. Without Mac, a distraction or some source of safety, it felt impossible not to hurt myself. It seemed obvious to me that I was suffering, but somehow, others missed it. Most of the time, I felt like I was screaming for help, but all that came out was silence. I always managed to cover up my darkness and my cuts. It was a skill, but I still have one faint scar on my left arm. I felt proud of this scar for a long time because it was the only time I managed to cut deep enough that the amount of blood scared me. Shedding blood and breaking skin is a loud and clear message that could be avoided if we listened more carefully. Energetic communication has different volumes, and usually, once someone is screaming, it's because they haven't been heard yet. I was used to feeling invisible in my pain, living in a world where I noticed so much that others didn't. I chose animal friends whose sensitivity reflected my own, and when we were together, we felt heard and seen. Every summer, leaving Mac meant returning to a state where screaming was the only form of efficient communication if I wanted to be heard.

Back in Malaysia, home alone and felt scared, I would turn on all of the lights in our apartment, walk around with heavy footsteps and yell, "I am home and I am not afraid of you. If you are hiding from me, come out and face me. I am home, and you are not invited to be here. I am not afraid of you!" I walked up and down the creaky spiral staircase, in and out of every room, as if I was surveying the perimeter like a guard dog, declaring my presence and evacuating any energies that were not invited into our house. I tried my best to maintain a sense of strength and fearlessness, despite an underlying tremble in my breath. There was something about this ritual that made me feel safe. I don't even know what or whom I was yelling at though.

A couple of months after I started doing this, we were robbed. Our mum saved us, when she saw the strange man creeping around downstairs in the middle of the night. She locked eyes with him and yelled bloody murder until he bolted out the way he came. That unwavering maternal instinct kicked in when she realised that her kids were in danger, and she was ready to draw blood. A few days later, while my brother and I were playing cops and robbers in the jungle (without noticing the irony until now), we stumbled upon an abandoned campsite on top of one of the mountains near our apartment building. Amongst empty soda cans, broken bottles, and plastic bags, we found my jewelry and other trinkets from our home. We realised that from this location, you could see directly into all of our apartment windows. They were watching us all of the time, waiting for the right moment to come, waiting for us to fall asleep. They were learning our patterns and getting to know us from afar. I felt them. I didn't know how I knew someone was watching me; I wasn't aware of intuition or the details of my gifts at that point, but I knew that I felt something strange.

The night that we were robbed my dad wasn't home. He was away, as usual. This wasn't the first time that we were in a compromised situation in a foreign country, and my mum was left alone to defend and protect the family. This wasn't the first time that I noticed the impact of his absence. I didn't sleep for months after we got robbed, and my mum started sleeping with an armoury of baseball bats, tennis rackets, and other miscellaneous sports equipment by her bed. Our safety was in her hands.

I have since learned that safety is an illusion. There is no such thing as complete safety, and it is all a construct of our mind. It's impossible for us to ever truly be safe, from a logical perspective. Even if you do wear a seat-belt, you can still be fatally injured in a crash. When we rely on something outside of ourselves to be our source of anything, we create an unnatural imbalance that will ultimately need to be energetically recorrected. It would be like holding the string of the bow and arrow back forever and never releasing the tension. When you attach something unnatural to the natural world, it will ultimately be taken over and destroyed in time. Safety is unnatural. In the natural world, there is no such thing as safety. Just as the horses move in response to the coyote's presence, they can never guarantee their safety from predators. Even when a baby is in their mother's womb, they are not completely "safe" or protected from life. Life continues to occur and it brings what it brings into that baby's life. The only time we are truly safe is when we aren't focused on safety. Because safety is a construct of the mind, when we focus on it, or the lack of it, it becomes present in our reality, or at the very least, its fragility does.

There is always something out there, or inside of us, that poses a threat to our survival. No matter how close Mac and I became and how much time I spent with him, my mum always feared that he would hurt me. I suppose his sheer size was a logical reason for it. I never wore a helmet, despite riding him bareback with a lead shank cleverly tied around his neck to control him. I felt safer with him when there was little to nothing between us. I trusted him with my life and he never let me down. Our intuition and emotional connection is what kept me safe. I was always extremely aware of what was going on for Mac, learning his language through experience and sensation. I knew when he was on edge and I always knew right before he would have a reaction like he did that one day with Melinda. I'm sure there were times when I seemed reckless in how I was with Mac, galloping in the back field with no bridle or saddle, or swimming in the lake on his back, but I think I was safe because of our intuitive bond and communication. I respected him, and he respected me. If I bought into my mum's fear, or stopped listening to Mac, I could've easily put myself in danger.

How do you manage your pain and emotions as a child?

Were there times in your life when you felt lost and stuck?

Did you feel overly sensitive, and did you feel understood?

If you felt fully supported to be yourself, who would you be?

What did you crave more of as a kid?

What felt like it was missing from your life?

What were your most dominant feelings and reactions/behaviours growing up?

How did you express yourself as a kid?

What do you see as your source of safety?

When do you feel unsafe in life?

What does safety feel like?

Are we ever really safe?

What if you were your source of safety?

CHAPTER 8

FITTING INTO SMALL SPACES

"You have been taught your legs are a pit stop
for men that need a place to rest
a vacant body empty enough for guests
but no one ever comes and is willing to stay."
- RUPI KAUR

I grew up in a man's world from Malaysia to Dubai. Having spent a large chunk of my life in a deeply patriarchal environment, I learned the roles women should play in order to survive, and I was often drawn to people and partners who held that same energy.

Sexuality is so often hidden in the darkness. When I finally took Sex-Ed in fifth grade, we didn't learn about intimacy, pleasure, or the emotional side of sex. It was all scientific diagrams, reproductive systems, and birth control. Everyone in the classroom was uncomfortable, including the teacher. It was a semester filled with cringing, laughing, and passing notes. At this point, I was already deep in my own inner exploration, but it was all very private. I hadn't yet had sex, but I was connected to self pleasure and exploring my own body. Sex always seemed like this forbidden act that no one talked about but everyone thought about. I felt their thoughts.

When I was six, I would play on my wooden rocking horse that had brown leather straps to hold onto and a raggedy brown mane and tail. I had it since I was three years old; it was my version of a safety blanket. It was one of the things that my parents brought from Calgary to Malaysia when we moved to create a sense of familiarity in an incredibly unfamiliar place. I remember one day I realised that when I rocked on the wooden back of the horse, I felt something really good, like a wave of pleasurable heat washing over my entire body. I felt it in the roots of my body, and the more I pushed and rocked back and forth, the better it felt. I stayed in my room for hours after, wondering what I had just experienced, and why I felt that I had done something wrong. I felt like I needed to hide, just in case my family could sense what I had done. I had a secret.

When I was seven, my brother and I were playing doctor with our friend. His name was Gianni. He thought it was a good idea for us to take things from the game to real life. He nominated himself as the doctor and I was the patient. I suppose my brother was the nurse. Gianni had beautiful dark, thick eyebrows, and he was about a year older than my brother and three years older than me. He felt like a bully, and I kinda liked him. As he brushed his hands up and down my limbs, I felt a tingle of energy rush down my back towards my root. I hoped that he thought I was pretty, and that he was enjoying this exploration as much as I was. I felt safe to lie down, close my eyes and allow it, knowing that my big brother was there to protect me. Gianni started to move towards my abdomen, just as you do in the doctor game, tracing the lines of the body. I followed the sensation of his hands walking around my body, wondering where he was going next as they migrated off. I was scared to open my eyes to find out what he was doing or where he had gone. His hand suddenly reappeared, holding the zipper at the front of my swimsuit, and it dragged down towards my root, unzipping me and exposing my body. My brother immediately told him off, and I jumped up and ran home, disguising the waterfall of tears that fell down my face. Whatever he did, it felt wrong. We stopped seeing Gianni after that.

Just like everything else, sexual trauma and shame travels through the bloodlines of families. If it goes unnoticed and unprocessed, it stays hidden in the blood, growing in its power. I could never quite understand why I felt the way that I did about sex. It felt more like a tool of control than an expression of love and connection. It was a symbol of power. Letting your guard down and truly surrendering to intimacy seemed like a foolish thing to do. It only ever ended in chaos and heartbreak. When I look down the line of my family, I quickly see that sexless relationships are the norm. I always felt that there was more to it than statements like "I'm just not a very sexual person" or "we don't sync up sexually." I also see that sexual trauma and physical abuse lives in my family's blood.

Men always watched me in Asia. I always attributed it to my shiny blonde hair, white skin, and big bluish, green eyes. Perhaps I was an image of wealth and opportunity, or perhaps I looked like the women in the movies. They always wanted to take pictures with me, and sometimes they called me "Hilary Duff," which at the time, I secretly loved. When I pranced through the malls, I felt their hungry eyes undressing me and burning deep holes in my back. It was common for men in Malaysia to purse their lips together and suck in, making an obnoxious kissing noise to get my attention. One time, when I was walking to the market from school, I spotted a man standing underneath the cement bridge pleasuring himself as he watched me walk by. I felt a mix of discomfort and pride. His strange fixed gawk displayed his desire for me, and something about that pleased me.

From a young age, I learned that my worth was measured, consciously or subconsciously, by how much men desired me, how much they liked me, and how much attention they gave me. My worth lived in my physical appearance and how agreeable, attractive, and easygoing I was. Something that used to motivate me around boys and men was competition. If there was another woman involved, I would do anything to get him. It became more important to get the guy than anything else. That is all I cared about. I've even at times had the desire to steal men from their partners. I would have absolutely no remorse about it either. It was as if I knew that if men chose me over their women it was the ultimate display of desire. It was the ultimate display of my worth. If a man would choose me over his wife or girlfriend or another girl who had his eye, it must mean that I was the ultimate girl. Most desirable. Most beautiful. Perfect.

When I was a teenager, I kept a list of all of the boys that I hooked up with. This list felt important—proof of something. When I would return home from a sexual escapade, I would excitedly write their name onto the list while counting how many names there were. When I reached high school, this list transformed from boys that I hooked up with to boys that I slept with—proof of my worth, my shield of protection.

My first time having sex was one I mixed up between two men, both of whom I didn't actually like or want. I tend to dance between who was actually my first. I think I know who it was, but I tried to forget him and what happened. He was Turkish, around five to six years older than me, and we had nothing in common. That's typically how it goes, right? We met in the club in Bangsar on a weeknight. He had eyes for me, and I accepted them. I craved the attention that he, or any man, gave me.

I wanted to be seen. A few weeks after meeting, and after several hot and heavy dance floor makeout sessions, he invited me to his house. He lived near us in a local part of the neighbourhood. Our family driver, Sharil, drove me and parked outside the house to wait for me as he always did.

The sky's darkness provided the perfect backdrop for what was about to occur. The Turkish man grabbed my hand and pulled me into his house. His slimy grin exposed his jagged teeth which sat below his barely there black mustache. It felt dirty and unkempt. His house was dark and lifeless. I was surprised to see his parents sitting on a small, dull grey couch in the left corner of the main room. They smiled, and his dad waved at me, grinning a similar slimy grin. It felt strange and unfamiliar. They didn't speak any English. The only decorations on the wall were Turkish confederate flags. His dad wore the same suspicious 'stache. The guy I was there for pulled me up the narrow, cave-like staircase and led me into his bedroom. He was gentle in ways and forceful in others. I felt the mugginess of their house on my skin. His bedroom was just as boring and uninviting as the rest of the house—colourless. Confederate posters with text in Turkish plastered his walls. The screen on his desk was lit up and MSN was open. I pictured him sitting there on the black, plastic IKEA chair, chatting with me. My stomach flipped. He grabbed a thin brown blanket from his bed and laid it on the hard floor, motioning for us to meet there. His laugh was more like a cheeky chuckle, one you'd expect to hear out of someone socially awkward. We barely spoke; most of our communication was done through MSN, texting, or body language. His movements were also awkward; he moved his hands up and down my body at a rapid pace. It was clear he wasn't looking for something slow and sensual. He approached me the same way an eager child would a Christmas present—with anticipation and a lack of control. He began to stick his long and thin tongue into my mouth. I accepted it. The only thing that truly attracted me to him was his deep and intense desire for me. He unzipped my jean shorts and pulled them down to my feet. He reached towards me like a child reaches into a candy box. When he entered me, I felt a mix of satisfaction and confusion. The moment it happened, I felt powerful in knowing that I was no longer a virgin. I felt safe in his desire, and I felt unsafe in the rest of the reality. It was unmemorable, stale, and the type of event I wanted to forget. I wondered if we both used each other. Did he really like me, or just the idea of me? I didn't want anyone to know about it. All I wanted them to know was that I was no longer a virgin. I was no longer inexperienced and vulnerable. I had taken care of it before someone else could.

The next guy who played with my mind was 20 years older than me, and I was 14 when we first met. It felt like we came close to being intimate when we sat at the fire pit one night playing chubby bunny with marshmallows or when we were snuggled up on the couch late one night watching a movie in his house. Whenever a sex or intimate scene came on the screen, I felt the heat of desire blast through the house. I felt aching in my groin. I wanted to feel what it felt like to be with him. I wanted to feel his desire for me. I knew what he wanted from women; I could tell by the various MAXIM posters in his garage plastered on his walls with naked women. I knew what it felt like to feel a man's desires through his eyes, and they were there. He fixed what my dad couldn't in the house; he helped my mum when my dad wouldn't. He knew that I was suffering. He never gave me what I wanted, and no matter how much he did give my family and I, it was never enough. It was never exactly what I wanted, but he came close. He played the role of being a safe and reliable man in my life perfectly. Even though he didn't really understand me, he was always there when I needed him and always showed up.

Later, I flirted with danger in Bali. There he was across the club, the danger and attention I had been looking for. His ocean blue eyes and fiery auburn ringlets were unmistakable in a crowd. Everything about him seemed to have been created to lure me in: a beautiful predator. The moment my brother saw him, I felt the temperature of my blood rise. He didn't like Jordan. He didn't trust him. Knowing how much my brother didn't like him made him all the more alluring to me. He was my perfect prey. And I was his.

After several drinks, Jordan gave me a look and pulled my hand toward the back door of the club. Before anyone (including my worried brother) would notice, Jordan picked me up into his arms and wrapped one hand around my leg, beside my groin. We had already kissed inside while dancing, but what was about to take place was much more than that. I felt an intense desire pulse through my veins. Jordan wasn't the type of guy who didn't get what he wanted, and he used force to make it happen. This wasn't the first time I had felt this type of control with a man, and the truth was, I wanted it. I felt safe knowing that this man wanted to control me, and he knew how to.

We slipped onto his motorbike and made our way down the streets of Kuta to his beach shack. As we drove, Jordan kept one hand on my thigh, holding me down. His house was small: one room and the walls were decorated with surfboards. Jordan was a man of little words and almost everything was spoken through eye contact and body language. He threw me onto his unmade bed and jumped on top of me. I loved feeling the heat of his body on me as he moved up and down my body, covering me in his saliva. I felt the hot bulge in his groin, and something inside of me shifted. As he continued his play, making his way to his entry point, I put my hand down towards his groin and whispered, "Not tonight" in his ear. As I said, Jordan wasn't one to be told what to do. He did what he wanted, when he wanted. I remembered being told at one point that he and his brothers were in some way royal. In Malaysia, this wasn't exactly a surprise.

   He continued to kiss and lick me, and I said again, "Babe, not tonight," as I felt his hand reach toward my panties. At this point, something in him had shifted. He wasn't used to being told no; he didn't like it. He looked up at me, his green eyes revealed specks of darkness. "What do you mean?" At this point, I don't know why or if it was true, but I said, "Because it would be messy." I looked up at him, speaking his language with my eyes. "Fuck, girl, why didn't you say before we left the club?!" He responded with a strike of frustration. "I'm sorry, I just realised." "I don't really care, let's do it anyways!" The truth is that I had had "messy sex" before and didn't mind, with the right person, but suddenly, even with vodka and diet Red Bull pulsing through my veins, he didn't feel right.

   I got up from the bed and walked to the bathroom. When I returned, he had already fallen asleep. I was no longer of use to him. He was done with me. At this point, it was the early hours of the morning, and I didn't know where I was or how to get home. I was deep in the streets of Indonesia, way off the main drag of Kuta, and I seem to have remembered that the motorbike ride over was at least 10 minutes (which, in Bali, means a lot). I decided to climb into bed with him and figure it out in a few hours. I woke up a few hours later to a bang at the door. "Bro, let's go. Surf is up!"

I decided to cuddle up to him with hope that he would stay with me and maybe drive me home later. The truth was that I still wanted him to want me. I wanted him to give me worth; I wanted to be good in his eyes. I wanted him to like me. He allowed me to cuddle him for about two minutes, before he pushed my hands off of his torso and jumped out of bed. As he pulled on a semi-dry pair of boardshorts from the floor and grabbed one of the surfboards on the wall, he looked up at me and said, "I'm going surfing; you can leave whenever." I sat there, positioning myself in a way that felt most sexy, hoping that he would offer me a ride home. Instead of getting what I wanted, he turned to the door and said goodbye. The truth is, the blood of my ancestors saved me. The heavy flow of their magic and wisdom put a stop to him entering my cave. He was not allowed inside of me. Despite my dark wishes, he would never enter the gates of my palace.

I lay in his bed for a few minutes, thinking about my decision. There was a huge part of me that wished that I had let him in. I wanted him. I wanted to be seen. And I wanted him to want me. I wanted him to like me. I thought about heading to the beach and giving him another opportunity. I thought about giving him what he wanted, so that he would stay with me. In some strange way, I felt safe with him and the power that he held. I thought about what it would be like to be his woman under his control. I stayed in his bedroom for an hour day-dreaming about this alluring life, before I finally made my way back to my brother's villa to face his wrath.

A few months after that trip to Bali, I experienced the scariest moment of my life. It was the first time that I became aware of how careless I was being with my life. That was one of the first times I realised I was putting myself in danger. The truth is that I had no business being in Thailand. The months leading up to that trip, and the end of senior year, were spent in bed hiding away from the world and slowly erasing myself.

> "I'm not for everyone,
> but who I am for, I'm for in a major way."
> – LALAH DELIA

I was deep in the throes of an eating disorder and depression and was at my wits' end of believing in myself. I had pushed any help away and made helping myself feel like an impossible task.

It was the second night of our trip. The boys were all staying in a house together about 20 minutes from us. We were staying in a hotel with the rest of our grade. Our group of girls decided to drive our scooters to a half moon party that we had heard about. We were already pretty drunk when we drove our scooters under the night sky on the local roads. On trips like these, I was pretty much permanently drunk. I barely ate, and when I did, I purged it up. My friends all knew, but at this point, I was somewhat of a broken record. When we arrived at the party, a few of us immediately noticed this guy. He was shirtless and had shoulder-length brown, thick, curly hair. He ran his manly, muscular hands through his hair, slicking it back like they do in male model commercials. His perfectly toned torso glistened with sweat, reflecting the light of the moon. He was tall and had a bit of a Tarzan-meets-beach-boy vibe. We all wanted him. I was going to get him.

Within minutes, I had caught his eye. He and I left the party, hopped on his bike and made our way to the beach. My friends were mad at me, but I didn't care. My focus was elsewhere. We spent a few hours making out in the ocean and swapping stories and drinking vodka coolers that we grabbed from the local 7-11. He invited me back to his place, which was just a mile down the beach. Once we got to his place, I began to feel off. Something wasn't right. I ignored what I was feeling, untied my fire-red triangle bikini top and climbed into bed with him. Although I didn't feel safe, there was something about his warm, big, manly body that felt comforting as I held tightly onto him. I wanted to be as close to him as I possibly could.

While we were having sex, the front door to the wooden, air-conditionless chalet opened. Instead of jumping up to protect me, he leaned back, crossing his arms behind his neck, as if to display his work. "Hey, bud," he said nonchalantly to the mysterious man who stood in the door frame. This man scared me. His eyes were dark, and the way he stood there looking at me like I was fresh catch didn't feel right. "That looks fun, can I join?" His friend dropped a baggy of white stuff on the bed and sat at the edge, waiting for his friend's permission. Ed smiled and shrugged his shoulders, passing me off. My mind told me to keep it cool and go with it, but a voice appeared in my head and calmly said, "Run, Chloe!" I pulled the cheap hostel bed sheet up around my exposed chest, grabbed my bikini top and bottoms, and told Ed from Edmonton that I needed to go to the bathroom. I didn't have a plan, but I followed the strange, familiar voice in my head. The bathroom had a small window, and even though I was worried that they would be mad with me or not like me anymore, I propped it open and climbed out.

It was around 6 a.m., and the sun was just starting to rise. I somehow recollected how to get out of the hostel that Ed was staying at and made my way onto the main beach road. I had no idea where I was going, had very little money, and my phone was dead. I flagged a cab, and when he rolled down the window, I realised that I had no idea what the name of our hotel was, or where it was. My mind was blank. The cab driver got impatient and drove away. I started to freak out. I was scared that Ed's friend would come and find me, so I started to run. I was wearing a barely there black denim skirt and a sheer black halter top covering my fire-red bikini. I decided to pull over another cab when a name dropped into my mind. I gave him the name, taking a breath as he turned his head nodding. Getting into that cab felt like a small win. Maybe I was safe, and maybe I was on my way home. We drove for about 20 minutes when I realised that we were not anywhere I recognised. He pulled over and said the name that I had given him. I gave him the little money I had left and started to cry. He yelled at me and drove away, snarling something under his breath which no doubt meant, "stupid white girl." I felt like a stupid white girl. I was never going to see my friends again or my family. I was alone. I had taken myself to the extreme and gambled with my life. I felt invincible in my carelessness, and as a result, I was going to probably get kidnapped or raped or die of starvation. I was terrified. I even thought about going back to Ed's place. Maybe I would be safe with him and his friend? I was so angry with myself; I should've stayed there with him and just gone along with it. Now I was somewhere in the mountains of Koh Samui.

That same voice that told me to get out of Ed's chalet popped back in my head and said a word. It was the name of the house where the boys from my school were staying. I couldn't believe it. Where did that come from? This time, I flagged down a guy on a motorbike, and asked him if he wouldn't mind driving me to the house. He had a friendly face, and something inside of me told me to trust him. I hopped on the back of his bike and he drove me to the house, which was only two minutes from where I was. When I saw that house, I started laughing and crying as I ran to the door. I couldn't believe I had made it.

Men were my escape and they were my drug. They gave me the attention I didn't get in my family, and they made me feel wanted and seen, a temporary fix. There was always something so satiating about being able to reach out to a man and feel like they cared. I had pretty hefty back pockets of men. I collected them and kept them there for times when I needed some satiating. I felt lost. Before accepting both my dark and my light, my relationships had always been either short, chaotic, and passionate, or long, uncomfortable, and confusing. Every relationship involved some form of lying and cheating.

I was always looking for trouble and somehow getting away with it. When we grow up in trauma, our world continues to bring similar experiences into our life, guiding us to heal what is underneath the surface. Until we face what we are running from, we will keep running. I never felt safe, and so I subconsciously continued to create things in my life to show me that. I continued to play with fire when it came to men, for several years after high school. It took me some time, and a lot of broken hearts to really understand that men were not my source. As long as I continued to look for love, safety and worth in men, I would continue to walk the line of chaos and pain with them.

A few years after graduating from high school, I was driving through the majestic Albertan Rockies with my mum just before dawn. It was dark and shadowy, and I was listening to a podcast episode with Oprah and Paolo Coehlo. Just as Paolo was sharing about the importance of omens in nature, a large silvery grey wolf dashed out from the woods. I saw it sit along the road as my car flashed by in the twilight. The wolf stood stoically watching us pass. Her face was to the sky, looking towards the last remnants of the moon before the sun took over. She turned to face me, lasering her golden eyes into mine. I had been trained for many years to do what was right, accept the "light" parts of myself—go to school, do well, get the grades, look good, please others, please men, but when I saw this wolf, I forgot all about my confined way of living. She reminded me of something else, something wild and magical. Part of me wondered if she was real, or something that I was seeing that others couldn't. There was something the wolf embodied that I wanted, I craved. I turned to my mum and asked if she had seen the wolf standing by the road. She hadn't. I knew she was a message just for me. This wasn't the first time that I received a message from my animal guides, but it was one that still burns in my memory. I thought about the encounter for months after, replaying her glistening eyes in my mind so many times that I really began to question if she was real. My logical mind told me that it was unlikely, given that wolves are close to extinction and I had never seen one in the wild before. Something else inside of me asked me to trust and believe.

What happens when we lock eyes with a stranger? What is the part of us that gets activated when someone sees us? What is it that makes us desire to be desired? Is it simply being seen in a world where many go unseen? If we allow our sexual desire to lead us, will it take us to a place of deep satisfaction and connection, or will it take us to emptiness? In the same way, if we buy everything that we desire, do we end up feeling empty with too many things, or completely satisfied? I used to think that it was the men I was chasing and their desire for me, but now I think it was more the chaos that they brought with them. When I tethered myself to the highs of their desire, and looked for their eyes on me, I lost myself. The electricity that I felt and chased was deadly. It disarmed me, pulled me further away from my intuition and embedded me in my ego. It wasn't connection, it was disconnection. It wasn't safe, it was dangerous. It was self-destruction.

Which type of partners have you been drawn to in your life?

What patterns do you notice in the partners you've been with in your life?

What have been your relationship patterns?

What have you been looking for?

What have you run from?

What have you been scared of?

What have your relationships taught you about yourself?

When conflict arises in your relationships, how do you respond?

Do you show the people you date both your dark and light?

How do you define dark and light in the context of relationships?

"During this part of the journey,
the woman begins her descent.
It may involve a seemingly
endless period of wandering, grief, and rage;
of dethroning kings;
of looking for the lost pieces of herself
and meeting the dark feminine.
It may take weeks, months, or years,
and for many it may involve
a time of voluntary isolation—a period of darkness and silence
and of learning the art of deeply listening
once again to self:
of being instead of doing.
The outer world may see this as a depression
and a period of stasis.
Family, friends, and work associates implore
our heroine to "get on with it."
- MAUREEN MURDOCK, THE HEROINE'S JOURNEY

CHAPTER 9

SOLACE

"I hope you will go out and let stories, that is life, happen to you, and that you will work with these stories...water them with your blood and tears and your laughter till they bloom, till you yourself burst into bloom."

- CLARISSA PINKOLA ESTÉS

Nothing and no one were enough for what I needed in my times of darkness—the dark moments when I was lying on the floor, desperately alone, fading away into a skeletal frame and injuring myself. The times I found company with men who wanted nothing but my body or for me to play a part in their stories. It felt dark, and no one was enough to pull me out, except myself.

I needed to be held in the arms of someone who wouldn't disappear right in front of me the moment I started to trust them. I needed someone who understood what I was going through and could guide me through it while holding my hand. I needed a break from the noise inside my head. I needed time to heal. I needed to listen to myself to have a greater understanding of the power I held within me. I needed my intuition. What I craved most was a love that I could only find within.

There was nothing wrong with me. I came into this world feeling a lot with no understanding of why. There was no one to guide me through the darkness that I knew and felt in my blood. I was going through an initiation of sorts—learning to stand in darkness and be with it without wincing or shying away. There have been many who have come before me to stand in the same darkness. In a way, I am standing on their shoulders, walking within their footsteps and feeling what they once felt. I am learning to see the unseen and to feel beyond the barriers of the mind and societal restrictions. This is not something I can be taught in school. I must find my way through this forgotten forest. At times, I feel alone and misunderstood exploring this forest, and I want myself to know that those feelings are a part of it. I am not alone. We are not alone. Our intuition will keep us alive when we are in danger or straying far from our path. It's here to remind us that we are powerful and that we have chosen to be here. It will connect us with the people and experiences that we need in order to remember ourselves.

Soon we will realise that our bodies are not the enemy. Soon we will realise that our fight against our body, or any part of who we are, is a fight against our power. We will spend some time searching for our truth—while partially listening to our intuition—and it will take us to many places outside of ourselves. That journey will be sprinkled with moments of clarity and insight—a dark pathway lit by candlelight. This journey will take a turn when we begin to realise that our body is a divine vessel, and it is here to be our partner. It will carry us through this lifetime and have our back unconditionally, no matter how we treat it and what we put it through. Part of the unconditional love that we crave is in giving us what we need, whether we know it or not. Sometimes what we want and what we need are two separate entities, one being led by love and the other by fear. We will take ourselves to the edge of extremes a few times over before we begin to feel and explore this. And when we're ready, a teacher will enter our life who introduces us to a conversation that is bigger than food, our body, our story, and our pain. This teacher may or may not be a living human, but they will help us open the door—a door that begins an entirely new journey of discovery and truth. At this point, everything will change. As our lens re-fragments, we will see things differently. We will understand things differently. We will see the world differently. At times, we will feel like a sober person at a party full of drunk people. We will feel like we are withholding a secret. What once caused us incredible pain will feel neutral and blissful. What once felt insurmountable will become a powerful memory. We will break free from the matrix of limitation and fear. We will see beyond the concept of duality and separation, and we will begin to feel the connection. We will return to the wisdom and divine knowing of our divine self—the one who we entered this life as. Intuition is the key to unlocking our chains.

Have you written a letter to your younger self before?

What would you say?

What did you need?

How can you love that part of you?

Looking back, can you see the gifts that were hiding in the shadows of your experience?

If you were to return to that time of pain, could you hold it and surround it with love and understanding?

If darkness is a catalyst of growth, what did the darkness in your life bring you?

"Yes
it is possible
to hate and love
someone at the same time
I do it to myself
everyday"
- RUPI KAUR

CHAPTER 10

IN BETWEEN WORLDS

"Your fate lives within you.
You only have to be brave enough to see it."
— MERIDA, "BRAVE" THE MOVIE

My healing didn't happen overnight. It took me some time to find my intuitive voice. Although it seemed like there were moments where I was lost on the map of my life without direction, I can now see that there was always a subliminal guide pointing me toward my north star. I was always on track, even though I felt astray.

Canada always felt more like home to me than the other places I lived, and so the moment I could return, I did. A few days after graduating from high school, I left Malaysia and spent the summer at the ranch before attending university in Vancouver. Most of the years at university, I continued to hide behind distractions and rebel from structure. This time, my life really was up to me and I had less to blame on my parents.

I was very good at pushing the limits, and my competitive personality befriended the edges of everything. I dabbled in drugs and continued to cheat on boyfriends. I skipped classes, missed exams, and unsuccessfully concealed an eating disorder from my friends and partners. Behind the scenes, my sensitivities were getting louder and my ability to ignore them was getting weaker. If I partied for a few days and binged, I would stay in my bedroom, locked away from the world for at least a week to recover. Balance was not my friend. Instead of acknowledging my feelings and allowing myself to feel, I denied them and shielded my vulnerability with a false feeling of invincibility. I hated my body, and the only time that I liked myself was when I was high or drunk or embedded in the destructive power of my ego. Unfortunately, the fall from that tower always ended with intense self hatred. The moments when I was left with just myself were agonizing. I continued to drag bulimia around with me like an old, ripped up childhood teddy bear. I didn't need it everyday, but when I did, it was there waiting for me.

When I graduated from university, I felt disoriented. The logical move was to apply for grad school in Clinical Counseling. Everytime I sat with the application, my mind went blank and I felt lifeless. I felt like

I was grabbing for something to feel right and nothing really did. My boyfriend at the time was a mechanical engineer, and sometimes I would go downtown with him in the morning to walk him to work. He worked at one of the flashy high-rise buildings in downtown Vancouver. We would join the morning hustle and bustle of people in suits, rushing to work like an army of ants. I felt out of place and envious, wishing that I could pull off a two piece suit complete with heels and a snazzy briefcase. I always wondered if my hips and legs would look as trim and sexy in the skin tight pencil skirts that some of the women wore. I wanted to fit in with them and feel important. I wanted to have purpose. I started reaching for something and found myself in fashion for a short time. I worked at Aritzia and applied for some salary fashion jobs. On the outside, I fit in. I knew how to play and look the part. But I was riddled with anxiety on the inside. I stopped sleeping and always felt strange and out of place. I was constantly worrying if people liked me and if my outfits were good enough. I didn't last on that path for very long.

Something began to guide me towards food and wellness. Even though my intuition was drowning in self-sabotage, it was there, and in rare moments, I felt it. Before I began to really notice the little voice inside, it was indirectly guiding me. My boyfriend, Mark, was a gifted home cook and spending time with him in the kitchen and cooking for others had begun to open my mind to a different relationship with food. I began to notice how different foods impacted me differently, which started the journey of connecting with my body in a more intuitive way. Instead of controlling how I felt with food, I began to notice how food shifted how I felt. My awareness of myself and how I was living my life, and treating myself, was beginning to change. Seeing how happy food made Mark and how much joy he received when he cooked for others shifted something in me. Even if it was a complex dinner for 30 people, he never seemed stressed or scared. He always embraced these invitations with an open heart and childlike curiosity. His confidence and with food and passion for cooking began to rub off on me. I loved Mark deeply and always will. When we met, we really fit together. He was just who I needed. As I began to grow and change, our differences outweighed my love for him. I began to crave more intimate time to have deep and emotional conversations, whereas he wanted to do more with more people. He was all about the daily adventure and I was beginning to crave more solitude and silence. Mark was always doing something, cooking, building, creating, climbing, snowboarding, or fishing, and he excelled at all of it. The end of our relationship was slightly chaotic but our love for each other somehow managed to remain intact and transform into a friendship. It took me a few years to really process what happened and to forgive myself for how I hurt him. Towards the end, we broke up and got back together a few times, and I developed emotional and physical relationships with other men. I had a hard time letting him go and I spent quite some time denying the truth: our romantic journey together was complete. This was one of those times where I was really faced with how challenging it can be to trust and follow your intuition. Our relationship made sense in most ways and my mind was desperate to keep us together. On paper, we were perfect.

I ended up studying to become a Holistic Nutritionist, which is when everything shifted. I enrolled in the course without really knowing anything about it. One day, after a co-worker at Whole Foods mentioned it to me out of the blue, I found myself on the phone with the school manager, Shayna. The next day I was in her office, and after 10 minutes of chatting, I had paid my deposit to start classes in a week. Even though in ways it didn't make sense and seemed slightly rushed, it also felt right. The moment I met Shayna, we felt like old friends reconnecting. Every interaction leading up to it was easy, inviting, and magnetising. The moment I walked into the school my mind felt quiet and my body felt safe, as if I was coming home. This was the first time that I had chosen to do something simply because I felt called to it, and it wasn't connected to anyone else. It was mine. A choice for me, about me. That year was a huge turning point in my life, a time where everything else outside of me slowed down and a new world was being created inside of me. I was changing. By healing my relationship with my body and beginning to listen to it for the first time, a light emerged. For years, I had been controlling my emotions with an eating disorder. It was effective until it wasn't. My desires for something different were building. It was becoming more challenging to ignore my intuition.

That year I met Jaisri, another elder who marked a point in my path. The moment I walked into her classroom on the first day, I felt a deep desire to know her and sit with her. Her thick rimmed archaic glasses and porcelain white bouncy hair instantly created a sense of comfort and intrigue. Her gentle and vulnerable laugh and tone of voice reminded me of my own grandmother. She was our Ayurveda teacher. She brought with her a deep passion and commitment to the subject and seemingly had no care for how passionate or purposeful she sounded. Within minutes of class starting she was laughing, speaking in Sanskrit, writing new words on the board, and eyeing us as if to say, "How can you not love this as much as I do?" She approached Ayurveda the way that Julia Child approached cooking.

On the second day of class, we were learning about doshas, and when we arrived at Pitta, she called me to come and stand at the front of class. I jumped forward, pretending to be shy. "Pita, pita, pita. Yup… see, look at her eyes. How big and deep they are." She stared down at me with her gigantic grandma glasses, grabbed my left hand from me, and placed her ancient fingers on the inside of my forearm, closing her eyes to read my pulse. "Yes, there we go! Quite a Pita pulse here. With a dash of Vata." I never missed a class with Jaisri, and I ended up taking extra classes with her too. With her, I felt seen and special. She saw in me what I was beginning to allow myself to see. I felt as though we had met before and meeting her again had sparked something in me.

Once I graduated as a Holistic Nutritionist, I began working with clients one on one. Something strange began to happen. During their intake sessions where I was collecting their health history, I began to feel, know, and hear information about them that they weren't mentioning themselves. One day, I was doing an intake with a new client, a teenage girl and her mother. On the drive over, my body felt off and swollen. A part of me wanted to cancel the session because I had this sudden unexplainable feeling of being fat and ugly. The moment I walked into their house, I kept feeling that the mother needed to step away and give her daughter and I some time alone. When I met the daughter, the unpleasant sensation in my body increased. The waistband of my stiff raw denim jeans began to dig into me, as if they had been miraculously tightened. As we sat at the kitchen table discussing food and meal plans, my throat tightened every time I asked the daughter a question. I could feel her holding her breath as the colour in her pastel cheeks reddened. Even though we carried on with the session, the voice in my head got louder and louder speaking the same sentence over and over again, "Ask her mum to go into the other room." I glanced around the kitchen, and noticed an intricate array of colour coded labels and systems of organisation in the perfectly spotless glass cupboards. I finally decided to politely ask her mum to leave, along with some feedback as to why it might be helpful. Fortunately, she begrudgingly agreed. The energy in the room shifted and the discomfort slowly softened. Instead of feeling like an investigator, I planted my feet firmly on the laminate floor, opened my mouth, and allowed myself to speak. The words that came out of my mouth were strung together to create a deeply sensitive space for the daughter to share and explore. As I spoke, I too listened to the wisdom that came through me. I could feel how sensitive this girl was and how much pain she was holding inside of her. Sitting with her, the energy around us felt like specks of dust dancing around my body from head to toe, stopping in certain areas to grab my attention. I could also feel that the mum was unintentionally creating a stressful environment for her, and that the rules and restrictions needed to be loosened for the girl to feel more at ease. We ended up speaking together for an hour at which point the mother rejoined us and we created a plan together that felt in harmony with both of them. I left their house feeling completely energised and full of joy. I couldn't exactly explain what happened, but it felt natural, easy, and fun.

Have you ever felt in between worlds in your life?

Do you allow yourself to follow the intuitive breadcrumbs, when you feel stuck?

Looking back at your life, can you see that you were always being guided, even when you felt lost?

When you think about the moments when things changed, do certain people stand out in terms of their influence and what they brought forward for you?

Have you ever really been lost?

CHAPTER 11

UNSHACKLING INTUITION

"Bone by bone, hair by hair, Wild Woman comes back."
- CLARISSA PINKOLA ESTÉS

I'm scared of what I might see.
I'm scared of what I might find out.
I'm scared of what I might already know.
I'm scared of what I might feel.

I was six years old when I first remember experiencing the power of my intuition, sitting on my bedroom floor holding my shoelaces and getting ready for school. Up until this moment, my connection and contact with the divine was all about scary spirits—feeling them, seeing them, and being extremely afraid of them. This moment was different. My excitement for the upcoming day of school was immediately diverted by a tunnel of energy that descended upon me like a spaceship landing. Suddenly, the weightless shoelaces in my hands quadrupled in weight, dropping to the floor like dumbbells. I reached my hands up towards my ears to protect them from my mum's voice which sounded as though she was yelling directly into my ear with a megaphone, despite the fact that she was actually calling out to me from the kitchen in a regular early morning tone. I closed my eyes and breathed quietly as if there was someone coming up behind me. I didn't want to be found or caught. I wanted to stay hidden from whatever it was that was coming towards me. Although my eyes were closed, I thought I saw a large white doorway appear in front of me, and I felt a magnet-like energy pulling me towards it.

I sat there, on the cold hardwood floor of our neo-Georgian apartment, waiting for what felt like hours. Waiting for whatever this was to pass. It took me some time to realize that I was safe and still sitting on the floor of my bedroom, and that my mum was yelling my name over and over again. We were going to be late for the bus. It was the first time this happened, but it certainly wasn't the last. It happened again when I was studying for my exams in university, and again when I was receiving an energetic healing, and again when I did a hypnotherapy session. It seemed to always happen when I was stressed out or afraid.

This powerful, intuitive sensory experience continued to happen for many years before I started working full-time as a psychic medium, and it took me many years before I was able to sit through it with a sense of calmness, understand what it was, and know that I was safe. Looking back, I feel like it was my intuition activating and my psychic senses opening. I sense that it was my guides and ancestors showing themselves to me. I also think that it was my emotions coming up to the surface and moving through me. Emotions are energy in motion, and when we really embrace that concept, we feel it.

Once intuition calls us, the way it called me, we don't feel like we have an option. Once we say "yes," it can be quite a tidal wave of energy. At times, it has felt like I was being chased by darkness. As I deepened in my sensitivity, the intensity of what I felt and noticed grew. When I was in my early 20s, I began to hear whispers about my psychic abilities. It was as if when my eating disorder healed, and my need to control my emotions and not feel them lifted, everything that was sitting dormant inside of me began to wake up. I began to notice the intuitive experiences I was having like when I was in my nutrition consultations.

That same summer, one sunny afternoon at the ranch, I was sitting on my colourful farmhouse-style bedding in the basement bedroom listening to a podcast show with a well-renowned medium, Colette Baron-Reid. She was offering spirit readings to guests, sharing messages from their past loved ones. As I listened closely to her deep, confident voice, I felt the ease of what she was doing. The rhythmic tone of her voice intrigued me. It felt as though I was listening to myself do the readings. A warm, comforting energy flowed through my body, filling my heart chakra and solar plexus with an ooze of love. My throat chakra was on fire as I listened to the words leave Collette's mouth, feeling as though they were leaving mine. For that short moment, I felt clear, confident, and sure that this was who I was. Even though I had yet to begin my work as a medium, my desire had begun. It was a remembering. Moments like this continued to happen for a few years. I would suddenly feel the ease and confidence of my psychic gifts. These moments were also surrounded by other moments of intense doubt and insecurity when I would question and deny everything. Even though the desire was there, there was an equal amount of unexplainable fear. Avoiding or pushing down your emotions is like trying to stop your body from having a bowel movement. You might be able to withstand the organic movement for some time, but eventually, something is going to happen. The longer you wait, the bigger the mess.

For a long time, I remember always holding back emotions. I didn't want anyone to see that I felt emotion. Whenever I felt something, I would try my best to hide and swallow it. Sometimes I would swallow and hold my breath to the point that I felt consumed with fear. Tears in my eyes or flushed cheeks were a sign of weakness and difference. It was always a challenge to swallow emotion, but I was willing to pass out in order to hide what was actually going on.

After being lost within the turmoil of my eating disorder for several years, a woman came into my life, and I was ready to listen to her. I had started to listen to myself, my intuition, but only sparingly. The few times I listened, it brought me to people like Divi. Dr. Divi was a medical doctor who offered various perspectives and schools of thought when it came to healing. I had never met a doctor whom I felt safe with, until meeting Divi. Her warmth and sense of childish joy and innocence permeated through the room. She felt both delicate and powerful—an ancient healer lived within her. There was a purity that I felt in her energy, as if she had little to no ego. Somehow I knew that she wouldn't judge me. Her office and appearance were slightly disheveled, which added to the humility and accessibility that she offered.

Up until meeting Dr. Divi, every person I sat with to heal focused on what was wrong with me. They would join me in focusing on and building my fear of food and weight gain. Instead of speaking about other topics, they would hone in on the thing that I had already spent too much time obsessing over. Instead of feeling held, I felt analysed, and I left sessions sometimes feeling worse and more broken than when I arrived.

I needed someone who was going to sit with me and explore the darkness that I had been both consumed by and was aggressively ignoring. I needed someone who could hold me and the energy around me without focusing on the aspects of my life that I was obsessed with. She offered a neutrality that I hadn't experienced. When I sat in that room with her, I felt safe and held in a way that I never experienced before. There was no agenda, and she seemed to know a lot about me from the moment we began. It took a few months before I even began to wonder what she was doing or how she was doing it. I later learned it was intuition.

As soon as we began working together, it was clear I had been living in a traumatised state up until now, and during that first hour together, I was finally safe. The first time we met, our time together was more medical—short and unfulfilling. Even though our time together was limited, there was something different about her presence. She wasn't "just" a doctor. There was something about her that felt safer, softer, and more supportive. She wasn't in a rush and she offered treatment options that lived outside of the standard medical model, without bias or persuasion.

The next time we met, it was a different setting and there was a completely different energy in the room. I felt as though I had walked through a portal. It wasn't medical at all. For most of the session, her eyes were closed and it seemed as though she was speaking to someone else. She referred to the person as "they," and I didn't question it. Everything that they said was accurate and most of the words that came through her mouth sparked something in my body and triggered a lot of tears. She was doing something different, and there was something about it that pulled me in. I needed to know who "they" were.

We were wrapping up, and I couldn't help but ask, "What about my eating disorder, are we going to talk about that?" I couldn't believe that in an entire hour, we wouldn't talk about the eating disorder which seemed to be at the core of everything—the reason why I was there. "We might get to it; we'll see where your guides take us," she responded with an unexpected level of clarity and confidence that I was not used to. She was so trusting, and her trust in the guides created a sense of safety that I had never felt before.

I continued working with Divi for a few years before I really began to dive into intuition. Our work took me on a deep journey into myself where I transformed my relationship with my body which opened up a whole new world for me emotionally. I began to see my body not as an expression of me to criticise and hate, but rather a spiritual home to honour. Once I no longer directed all of my energy against myself and my body, there was more space for a deeper discovery of what else was hiding beneath the surface. I began to work more with others on their health imbalances, the way I helped the daughter and mother. For some time, I worked specifically with women with eating disorders. I began to notice that my nutritional consults quickly shifted into counselling style sessions, and I knew things about my clients that they never shared. I gravitated towards the emotional part of the consults, minimising the amount of time I would spend on meal plans. I also began to notice that the people that were drawn to working with me lived in a lot of darkness and hid it. I rarely had a "simple" one and done type of client.

My work with Divi was slow and steady in some ways but underneath the surface so much was shifting. It took me a few years of running away, before I really dug in. Divi dropped subtle hints a few times about my intuition, and I decided to join some of her weekend workshops that were designed around building our intuition. While I was at the workshops, strange things began to happen as if the psychic energy was being amplified. I began to be surrounded by synchronicities and really started to feel magical.

It was late one night in Vancouver when I found myself on an intro call for Divi's next event, a retreat in Whistler. She was co-hosting with a woman called Lynnette Brown, who apparently was her coach. "That's right, y'all, we are doing an advanced intuition weekend in Whistler where we'll be diving into your psychic gifts." The moment I heard Lynnette's voice, something inside of me awoke. The twang in her fierce Southern accent vibrated in my ears, causing waves of curiosity to spring forward. Who was this woman? I was committed. I signed up for the retreat that week, and soon after I had a call with Lynnette. She called herself "the love Matriarch," and I believed her. I could hear the songs of birds singing in harmony as she spoke to me over Skype from her home in Texas. She knew me and she knew much about me, and I felt as though I knew her. It was a short call, but it was all I needed to know that I was making the right choice. In just a few weeks, I would be with her in Whistler, learning more about myself than I had in a lifetime.

Did you ever experience something strange as a kid that you could never explain?

What is your relationship with synchronicities and coincidences?

Do you allow yourself to acknowledge the magic that is around you?

What moments in your life stand out as times of big change?

CHAPTER 12

THE INITIATION

"The parts of us that crave to be special are the disintegrated parts that feel unseen by the divine."
- CHLOE ELGAR

"Chloe, you are so psychic!" Lynnette said showing her excitement and confidence, causing an unavoidable tsunami of emotion to bubble up and pour out my eyes. The streak of purple in her hair polarised my vision as I felt her maternal warmth and unconditional support stand with me. This is when everything changed for me. The moment I was told by someone who I deeply respected that I was psychic I felt seen. She knew what I always knew. The moment she said it, I realised that I had been holding my breath my whole life, waiting for someone to tell me the truth. We call events in life "synchronicities" and "coincidences" to devalue and demystify the magic and pull ourselves into our minds and out of our childlike wonder and imagination. It was time for me to reclaim the magic.

We were in the middle of the weekend workshop in Whistler, and during the break, I brought over a copy of my self-published cookbook for Lynnette as a gift and a thank you for hosting the retreat (and entering my life). It was the last day, and I was worried that I might never see her again. The thought of losing her fierce presence in my life felt impossible. I needed to work with her somehow. I signaled to her energetically that I wanted to give her something, and she called me over to her. I shuffled to the front of the room, trying my best to hide the lifetime of emotions that were bubbling up to the surface. As if she didn't know, I handed her the book, tears in my eyes, and said thank you. She hugged me, cocooning my body in her undeniable power as she expressed her love and gratitude for me in her unmistakable Texan accent. I was about to walk away, not wanting to take too much time for myself, when she grabbed my hand and pulled me back towards her. "Darlin', what's wrong?" she asked with that Southern slang again. Her eagle eyes probed into mine, transferring the message that I wasn't getting away with a lie this time. I let my breath and bubbles out and broke down into a puddle of tears. Amidst the emotion, the words stumbled out of my mouth, "I don't think I'm psychic." The moment I said it, I hoped with all of my heart that she would refute it. What I didn't know is that my saboteur was all over me and it was running this conversation. Shame, doubt, and fear were running the show. She giggled, wearing a large and slightly witchy smile, "Chloe, you are SO psychic!"

On the drive home from Whistler that afternoon, I couldn't shake this feeling that Lynnette was meant to be a bigger part of my life. There was something about her and how I felt when I was in her presence. She felt like family in a can't-put-my-finger-on-it kinda way. I suddenly felt a strong urge to email her immediately, before any more time passed. I worried that if I let too much time pass, she would forget me, and I would lose my chance to become the person that I felt inside. I pulled over, grabbed my phone, and sent the email. A few hours later, once I was home and spent way too much time refreshing my browser, her name popped onto my screen. She replied and said that something in her had her check her email, even though she was exhausted from the weekend and needed to go to bed. We started working together that week and have since become good friends. Her and her partner, Mike, are as close to family as you can get, without being blood.

It was after meeting Lynnette that I chose to return to the ranch alone and meet my ancestors for the first time. It was after meeting her, that I chose to turn my light on. The weekend that I met Lynnette was one of several seeds that had been planted in the same place. Everything prior to our meeting led me to her, but it wasn't until I heard those words come out of her mouth that the real work began. Meeting Lynnette was the true beginning of my psychic journey from a professional perspective. It was when I decided to acknowledge what I always felt and actually claim the label "psychic" publically. It was when I finally came out of the psychic closet.

That whole weekend in Whistler, I felt ravens were following me. Every time I went for a walk, or looked out the window, a group of ravens was there, staring at me. I always wondered why the world was so hard on animals like crows and ravens. I never quite understood it; their sense of mystery and trickery intrigued me. A flock of ravens is often called "unkindness," but I see ravens as messengers of magic and truth. They aren't unkind; they are formidable. On the last day, as I drove home to Vancouver through the mountains a raven flew alongside me, as if to remind me of what I now knew and what I needed to do. It was time to go into the dark and do the work. It was time to heal the parts of me that I had been hiding.

Seeing the flock of ravens in Whistler reminded me of my last drive home to Vancouver from the ranch earlier that year. It was just before dawn. I had already been driving for two hours and was nearing my favourite stretch of the drive deep in the mouth of the rocky mountains, surrounded by all of her wisdom and beauty. I crave the stillness and silence of the wild. This is where I feel safest and most at home in the world. It's a different type of alone when you're out in the wild. In a city I can feel so alone, living in a cement block sharing a wall with a stranger who is probably doing exactly as I am just a few meters from me. Both "alones" are an illusion. We are never alone; we are always surrounded by something—life or death. I prefer the sounds of crickets singing and birds talking, over the sirens and buzzing of power lines. I receive the most when I'm out in nature, between mountains. This is where I feel closest to me, my ancestors, and the oneness of life.

I decided to pull over, and let Ollie stretch his little legs. I jotted down some of the thoughts that were coming to me. There, waiting for me, were four large, dinosaur-like pitch-black ravens. Four, a number that reminds me of oneness and connection. Four, my favourite number.

The four elements of the world—earth, water, air, and fire. The four directions—East, South, West and North. As I opened the door of my white VW Rabbit, the ravens didn't move. They sat there at different points of the fence staring at me. We stared at each other. I waited to feel what they wanted me to know. Some say ravens and crows are omens, alerting us that something bad is going to happen. A tragedy is near. I don't see or feel that. I don't fear them. I speak to them, and listen to what they have to say. They remind me of who I am, and who we all are. I've always loved birds, and the more rooted I am in my magic, the more I notice birds and feel a connection with them. In many ways, ravens are the keepers of darkness. They embody the essence of darkness with so much confidence and clarity. They are perfect teachers for us to remember as we walk along the path of the wild. When we fear something, it's up to us to turn towards that fear and ask the questions that transform it from something outside of us to something that lives inside. They warn me not to forget and to hold the knowledge that we are all always connected. Our connection with the spirit world and other realms doesn't require a crystal ball or hours of meditation. It is here right now, just as we are. Once you've walked in the darkness, without a light, you can be with the dark without running away or running to someone. What I've come to realise is that my relationship with darkness is a powerful marker for where I am and how far I've come. Darkness is a truth test. When it confronts us, it brings up whatever we are hiding from ourselves, and if we are not ready, it can destabilize us.

Do you crave validation?

What would you do differently, if you had external confirmation?

Is there a part of you that feels psychic?

What if someone told you that you were psychic?

How would that change the way that you felt about yourself?

Have you ever met a person that you immediately felt that you knew and who knew you?

Do you believe in soul connections?

CHAPTER 13

THE VEIL

"There is nothing more important to true growth than realizing that you are not the voice of the mind - you are the one who hears it."
- MICHAEL SINGER

Two days after I got home from the retreat, a knock on my front door reverberated into my solar plexus like a kick in the gut. I raised my right hand into the air, signaling Ollie to stay on the couch and shuffled over to the door. My nerves were in my throat; I had spent the past thirty minutes attempting to calm the fear that filled the air of my apartment like thick black smoke. I was doing professional readings, and she was my last reading of the day. For some reason, I was more terrified of her than any of the others.

I opened the door, revealing an average height, middle-aged woman who seemed out-of-character for me. She was dressed in boring neutrals and wore a less than content smile on her face. As she walked through the threshold, I felt a grey cloud of energy enter in behind her. The alarm in my head grew when Ollie decided to stay on the couch rather than bounce towards my guest happily as he usually would. I had already done two readings today, but it was also the first day ever of doing paid readings in my life. Something about this woman told me that it was not going to be an easy hour. After 55 minutes of several "No, I don't feel that" and "That doesn't really resonate" comments, I gathered what was left of my fading confidence and closed up the session.

The moment she walked out of the door, seemingly unsatisfied, a dark cloud of smoke filled my apartment in seconds. "FAILURE!!!!!!!!" A familiar voice yelled at me in my head. "As if you thought you were a real psychic. Come on. What a joke. She is going to tell everyone that you failed, and that you are not the real deal. She is going to share it on instagram and everyone is going to see that you are a complete fraud!" I fell dramatically onto the floor, finding Ollie there by my side, nuzzling his wet snout under my left forearm. My end-of-life pity-party was disturbed by another unhappy thought, "Oh no, you are supposed to meet your web designer in 30 minutes at her office." "FUCK!" Should I cancel?" I sat there in between my choices for a few minutes, testing the after-taste of each option. I grabbed my phone to check if by some miracle she had emailed me to cancel herself. "BING!" A new email popped up, and it wasn't from my web designer. It was from Michael, no last name. I clicked on it, and my mouth dropped to the floor as my eyes blinked several times. "Hello Chloe, I was traversing avenues of light on the web in search of those whose essence enriches the spirit when I discovered your profound presence. You are one who connects to people in positive ways that inspire. I found everything of great worth and value. You are a pure source of energy. You should be very proud of what you are putting forth. It is with honour and respect that I write. Thank you for opening the gateway to your true self that all may experience the beauty and glory of who you are. I wish you a transformational path of sacred awareness. May you cultivate the love within you as you affirm awareness and may you investigate spiritual worlds as you benefit yourself and others. Do not give up. Yours in devotion and spirit, Michael, the ancient one."

I couldn't believe what I was reading. My logical mind told me it was spam, but my intuitive mind said it didn't matter. I wondered if it was Archangel Michael sending me a message through a communication channel. I remembered hearing someone share that our guides and divine support team will communicate to us in every way that they can, including through the internet and technology. Energy is energy. This was a message that I needed and it came at the right time. I realised that perhaps the lady who came for the reading didn't like what I told her, and she might not have been ready to hear it, but what I told her was the truth. I did my job. I went to my web design meeting that night, and the next day, I carried on with my readings as scheduled. I didn't give up.

We all have (at least) two voices in our head. Some call them fear and love, others call it ego and intuition. Divi referred to it as the mind voice and the soul voice. The first time I really noticed the different voices in my head was at a silent retreat in Maui in my mid-twenties. I was there with my mum, joining her on a week-long retreat with her Gurus, Eli Jaxon-Bear and Gangaji. Since it was a silent retreat, it would be the first time I hadn't spoken since I learned to speak. We were given clear instructions not to speak, write, or read for the whole week. We were being asked to travel deep within and discover what was actually going on within ourselves. We turned our phones and technology devices off and put them away for the week. We put away our books and journals, which I brought in anticipation to use during the retreat. Not talking and filling space with words created something entirely new for me. Like a chemistry experiment, closing the system meant that everything had to stay locked inside of me with nowhere else to go. Every day began with satsang and ended with satsang, and in between, we were left with ourselves. We were left with all of the noises inside of us. At first, it felt exciting and scary. The excitement about the challenge and the potential success—like finishing a juice cleanse or a 30-day push-up challenge. My mind loved the idea of testing its willpower and proving how strong I was. I soon realised that this experience wasn't a test and it wasn't about willpower. It was a choice instead of a challenge. I couldn't fail and I couldn't succeed. I was being invited to be with the one inside of me and witness. Everything we were told to do was merely presented as strong suggestions. There were no rules, and we weren't being monitored or watched. This week was up to us: our choice to honour silence.

It was the morning of the last day. Like every day in silence, I woke up extra early, excited to have coffee before getting ready for the day. I sat out in the back garden with my coffee and watched the waves coming and going. In and out. To the shore and then back out to sea. I rocked in my wooden chair, sipping on my slightly sweet, almond-creamed coffee. It was peaceful in most ways, and slightly alarming in others. There was a build-up of thoughts and energy in my head, and I really wanted to write them down. Unlike my times drowning in deep darkness, I was aware of my thoughts; I was aware of the build-up. I felt a familiar sense of condensed energy building in my body, and instead of doing something with the energy or getting away from it like I normally would, I noticed it. I stayed with it. I noticed more than I ever had before. I noticed it, because I had to. I was in silence. I was listening to the silence.

I hopped into the shower in hopes that the water would help to clear out some of the anxiety. As the hot water began to dance on my head and drip down my body, my energy began to shift, and I heard a soothing voice pop into my head, "Today, you will speak at the satsang." That morning, we attended the satsang meeting, and I observed others sit on stage with Gangaji sharing their experiences and asking questions. My hand burned throughout the hour, but I didn't go up. A few hours later, during the evening satsang, I felt a similar sensation in my hand. I had nothing to say, so I continued to witness others go up on stage. My hand suddenly shot up into the air like a hot air balloon, and Gangaji motioned for me to join her on stage. To this day, I have no idea what I said, but we sat together talking and laughing on stage for at least 10 minutes. When I sat down after, I felt joyous and clear.

The soul voice is our intuition. This is the voice that we are born with, and it embodies everything that is connected to oneness and unconditional love. The other voice, the mind voice, is a trained voice that is built over time. We are not born with a mind voice, and it takes time to increase in volume. The mind voice is connected to judgment, analysis, comparison, and logic. The mind voice centers around differentiation. It is connected to separation, the identity, and the ego. Neither are good or bad, and the truth is that they both have purpose. The mind voice is connected to fear and is in place to keep us safe. The mind voice can be brilliant and is a wonderful assistant in life if we work with it deliberately.

A mind without a master is a mind that runs the show and keeps you stuck, and a mind that is run by fear is chaotic and destructive.

Michael Singer speaks of this mind "voice" as your annoying roommate in his book Untethered Soul. He tells you to question this voice, and question its presence. When else do we willingly rent space in our mind, listen, and follow the words of someone who endlessly speaks so horribly to us? Once you pay attention to this voice in your head, you begin to wonder where it came from and whether it is actually you. This is the beginning of the journey into the self and into your awareness. Until we witness this voice, we are living unconsciously. This is the voice that I listened to for most of my adolescence. This voice is a trained voice, and it reflects all of the things that we have learned since birth. And when we move away from it, we begin to move towards our soul voice and our intuition. The intersection point of our mind voice and our soul voice is where emotion can be incredibly revealing. Emotion serves as an alarm signal, telling us that something is going on inside of us. Our emotion shows up as a sign that we are out of balance or in "split energy." Split energy is when we divide ourselves between the thoughts of our mind and the guidance of our soul. Typically it is when we have caught ourselves in a dilemma of right and wrong and good or bad. As soon as we go into this place of judgment, we disengage from our soul voice, which is a part of us that exists without judgment or criticism. I often say that the less sense something makes, the more intuitive it probably is. Our intuition is not governed by logic, and it exists outside of the mental mind (oftentimes referred to as the left brain).

In a book by Dr. Jill Bolte Taylor, called A Stroke of Insight, Bolte Taylor tells the story of how a blood vessel exploded in the left part of her brain, causing her to have a stroke. The revelations of her book created a big wave in the science world and offered a powerful introduction of

> "It is through science that we prove,
> but through intuition that we discover."
> - HENRI POINCARE

intuition to the masses, especially in the world of science. This woman, who is an expert in neuroscience, had a stroke in the left side of her brain, which silenced the part of her that believed she was separate from the world. It silenced her critical, detail-oriented, strategic mind and exaggerated the side of her brain that was connected to the sensory experience and being in the present moment. Instead of seeing herself as an individual, separate from the world around her, she suddenly saw a continuous, undivided connection. There was no ending or boundary between her body and what she saw around her. She suddenly felt incredibly expansive, connecting to the infinite energy of her soul. One of the most memorable parts of her experience was that the brain chatter and potential fear that she expected to hear was silenced. This experience was deeply profound for her as she had this powerful experience of connection and oneness, and it led her to expanding her research on the brain and spirituality. In her words, she woke up and recognised that the right side of the brain isn't well-developed or supported in our world.

Our world has been developed favouring the left brain. Critical thinking, problem-solving, and knowing the difference between right and wrong are all high on the list of educational standards for children. Math and science are prioritised over music or art, and careers rooted in the arts are seen as less than careers like law, finance, or medicine. Our imagination, which is the connection point to the psychic mind and our psychic senses, is brushed aside as childish and something to grow up from. And so we leave the "make believe" land and force ourselves to live in reality that we ultimately want to escape from. From a young age, we are taught that our emotions are an inconvenience and a source of vulnerability that must be hidden if we want to be successful and worthy. Essentially, we are taught not to listen to our intuition.

Most of us don't have an experience like Dr. Jill Bolte Taylor, where our fear-mind and brain chatter is spontaneously extinguished. When

I began to recognise my intuitive voice and also witness my mind voice, it didn't mean that things changed immediately. It took me a few years of spiritual work and daily practice to decrease the volume of my mind voice and create space in my mind to hear my intuition. It's not like once you notice it, it sorts itself out immediately. I had to work through all of the layers and years of not listening to myself and drowning out my intuition with fear and control. I had to excavate the deeply rooted beliefs that I wasn't worthy of being happy, loved, or experiencing ease. During these years, I experienced some moments of chaos and met my own version of "spiritual burnout." Now that I had acknowledged who I was and who I wanted to be, I had to learn how to be her and let go of all of the versions of "me" that I had collected along the way, for protection.

Have you acknowledged your intuitive voice?

Are you more of a logical or abstract thinker?

When you think of the concept of "oneness" how do you feel?

When you look at the world around you, do you feel connection or separation?

When do you feel separation or what do you feel separate from?

What does separation feel like for you?

CHAPTER 14

THE ILLUSIVE SHIELD

"She was safe when she let it go.
When she let it all go.
All of her beliefs about safety.
and who was supposed to make her feel safe.
They weren't her safety.
They weren't her source of anything.
She was.
And when she finally let it go,
the need for safety left with it."

– CHLOE ELGAR

"Come on babe, I really want to go to the Montane Mansions, and I think you're going to love it. We'll get such amazing photos for your instagram!" My husband, Faris, continued with his incessant plea which started a few days ago the moment we landed in Hong Kong. This wasn't the first time Faris would wear me out with his undying consistency. The problem was that I didn't really know why I didn't want to go; I just didn't. I knew it didn't make sense and probably seemed lazy. This wasn't my first rodeo with a logical, masculine mind. I grew up having these debates with my brother daily. I didn't want to go somewhere or meet someone, and I couldn't explain it rationally; I just felt it. My success rate at holding my ground up until this point was about 70 percent, despite the intense guilt trips I was gifted in exchange for listening to myself. Faris was yet to learn his lesson about not pushing me when my intuition was saying a loud and clear "no." I was still learning how to really hold my ground and trust what I felt, especially when it made no sense. We were staying in Hong Kong for a drawn-out layover on the way to Bali in December for our overdue honeymoon. I had managed to dodge visits to the Instagram famous Montane Mansions up until now.

In these moments when I feel a clear "no" in my body about going somewhere, it usually translates into not being able to put an outfit together, changing way too many times, and asking way too many insecure questions. The more I push past it and listen to guidance that comes from outside of me, the further away from myself I fall. I knew that Faris really wanted to go, and I didn't want to let him down. So we went. The moment we stepped out of the train station, I felt a strong pull to turn around. We kept walking. Miraculously, we bumped into one of my brother's closest friends from high school who I forgot lived in Hong Kong. He questioned why we were in this area. He stopped us in our tracks, confused. And yet, we kept going. The more steps forward my feet took, the more I felt as though I was leaving my body. We arrived at a large condominium structure that seemed to be the destination Faris was looking for. His eyes were buried in his phone, manically scrolling through influencer blogs to find the hidden entrance. Out of desperation to get this part of the trip over, his eyes darted towards a man who was walking through some double doors. Faris chose his entrance and dragged me by my hand; I felt a more intense pull to stay where I was. As the doors swung open, my stomach dropped to the floor of the cold, dirty laminate flooring. We had entered a very local, very chinese large butcher hall. Everywhere I looked there were dead animals, blood, and butcher knives on the walls and shelves. Faris took a deep breath, squeezed my already sweaty hand and once again pulled me forward. Once we made it out of the butcher hall, I thought I would feel better and lighter, but I felt worse. The heat in my hands had now transferred to my whole body, and I was covered in sweat. My heart beat was thumping in my ears and drumming through my jacket. We were now standing in the famous courtyard which sat in the middle of all of the crowded towers. What set these buildings apart was the fact that they were all attached, holding hundreds of units in each vertical tower. To some, especially architects and photographers, they were a wonder to marvel. For me, it was a tunnel and vortex of energy that I did not want to feel. I felt trapped and consumed. Faris looked towards the cement podium, where a line of influencers were attached, waiting for their turn to snap an iconic image. Faris pushed me towards the line. He meant well and he was unaware of the volcanic eruption of heat that was building in my body. I felt like every spirit of every person who has ever lived in these old buildings was surrounding me in a circle, waiting for their turn to talk. My Mouth felt full and my throat was tightening. The last girl, dressed in the cutest, but at the time, most annoying harajuku outfit hopped off the podium, motioning my turn. There was already a line of eager strangers waiting for me to grab my shot. I wanted Faris to understand and let me go home, but instead I felt his pressure and frustration with me. I wanted to please him, and I didn't want anyone to notice how difficult I was being. Why couldn't I be normal and why did I have to feel this? The moment I crawled onto the podium like a snail, the energy intensified. I was soaked in steamy sweat, but I was also freezing. All of my senses were exaggerated, and I felt everyone's eyes lasering painful holes into my body. Somehow, Faris continued to blurt directions out at me; his frustration was building in his voice. Tears began rushing down my red cheeks; I was embarrassed, upset, and scared, and I didn't really know why. I didn't feel safe there in my body or with Faris. No one could hear me or see me. The energy swept me off of the podium like a gust of wind, and I marched past Faris towards what felt like the actual exit of the courtyard from hell. Faris was upset with me, and I was even more upset with myself. We made our way back to the train station, tracing our previous steps without talking. I felt like I was going to either explode or disappear. I had been known to faint in situations like this, which I had on my mind. I could feel the energy around me circling like an angry storm, sucking everything into what felt like a dark drain. When we walked into the train station, the man beside me was rushing and bumped into a fellow train passenger who was walking in the other direction. Instead of having a calm interaction, the man threw his shopping cart at the other man and began yelling at him. They broke into a fight screaming at each other in mandarin. I couldn't believe it but also couldn't help but wonder if it was my creation. The world around us began to descend into chaos, and Faris realised that something wasn't right. His anger turned to worry, and he wrapped his arms around me as we made our way onto the train. When we got back to the hotel, I slept for 20 hours without waking. I was knocked out by the energy and all of the fear.

For a decent portion of my life, the biggest threat to my survival and happiness was myself. I was the one who ultimately made my choices and determined who was allowed into my life, and who wasn't. Our internal environment determines what shows up externally. As Abraham Hicks shares, our thoughts create our beliefs, which create our reality. My own fears and thoughts of not being or feeling safe were damaging to the reality that I lived. If I didn't feel safe, I wasn't safe and would continue to attract experiences that showed me that belief. We are hardwired for safety. Our most primal essence feels threatened when our foundation of comfort and security is being challenged. It takes constant practice to rewire our subconscious mind and to train our nervous system to feel safe in times of change, chaos, or crisis. The biggest belief that I had to purge was that men are my source of safety. I had to realise that believing in this, and seeking this, kept me out of my power and in resistance to my magic. In my relationship, the more that I focused on Faris being my source of safety, the less safe I felt. The more that my mind expected him to be a certain way for me, the less satisfied I felt with who he was being.

That same year, Faris and I went on a trip to Italy with my dad. We travelled for three weeks, drinking way too many aperol spritz, eating pizza, and exploring the towns of Tuscany. Spending this much time with my dad was a rare treat, and I soaked in his energy like a dehydrated sponge. During this trip, I encouraged myself to play the role of anthropologist and observe our relationship. I saw how much I craved his attention and his approval. I felt how desperate I was to feel his love and admiration for me. Time with him always felt so fleeting and holding on too tightly would make him disappear. It was interesting to be with him and my husband, Faris. The two men in my life, minus my brother Sam. I watched how my behaviour changed and how I began to once again focus on my appearance. The final test was the goodbye.

I felt it coming since the early hours of the morning, waking up to the bubblegum sunrise in my dad's friends' beautiful country house in Tuscany. Bubbles of emotion were building inside of me, creating a heavy pool of dread at the base of my solar plexus. I couldn't be present; my mind was already preparing me for the pain that was ahead. I wondered if everyone could see the invisible dark, shiny shield that was forming around my heart, protecting the deep and old wound of abandonment. Saying goodbye to my dad was a normal routine in my life, but it never got easier. Everytime it just ripped open the scab and dug deep into my raw flesh. When we got to the airport, my body began to shake and shiver as tears exploded from my eyes. As Faris and I traveled up the escalator to the departure lounge, I noticed my inner child reveal herself. I suddenly felt so unsafe and exposed as if I forgot to wear clothes and everyone could see me naked and vulnerable. I wanted to run away and hide. Once again, I had lost my protection.

Ingrid Kincaid, the rune woman, says that our obsession with safety is connected to our extreme aversion to death and darkness. If we fear death so deeply and fight so intensely to stay in the light, we are bound to meet our inevitable doom, sooner rather than later. As with anything, our childhood determines our relationship with safety—what we're taught about safety, whether or not we feel safe, and what we learn from observation. In my life, it was clear that my mum didn't feel safe, and her life continued to show her that. Even though there were many moments when her fierce maternal instincts kicked in, she had a hard time holding her ground and her power. She fostered a toxic story that men were her source of safety (physically, financially, emotionally), and because my dad was never fully there, she could never be safe for too long.

From the moment we leave the womb, our world opens up, as does the scope of what is possible for us to live through. I would argue that from birth onwards, I felt unsafe. A large part of this is because I felt the same fear that was in my mum, and most likely the women in our maternal line. So much of our relationship to safety is unconscious, passed on to us from our ancestors and their ancestors. We know now that there is a large distance between perceived threat and true threat. We also know that our mind and our fear response doesn't differentiate between a perceived threat (being chased by an imaginary panther) and a real threat (being robbed). So a lot of our fear around safety is about the unknown, the things that we can't control and that are unfamiliar.

As of yet in our culture, it is more familiar to hear, watch, and learn stories about women who were protected or saved by men. In my case, it is unfamiliar to leap into the unknown and trust that my partner would stand by me while I journeyed into my own darkness. Letting go of my idea of what safety is, was necessary to be able to actually get to real safety. The more I looked for what I needed in men, the less they gave it to me and the more unstable I felt. As my life reflected parts of my mum's more and more, I came to realise how important it was for me to change this. I needed to discover my sense of power and safety from within. I needed to stop searching outside of myself for what I needed to survive. I needed to stop supporting and building the story that my mum told me, which perhaps she learned from her mum. I needed to change something to begin healing parts of our family and lineage; this wasn't just about me.

Life will take you to a point that is beyond your conditioning. This is a point where you are in the unknown and you no longer have a road map of what to do or what not to do based on what you know and have known. There is that moment when we grow beyond our training and we are without the safety net that we've become comfortable with. At this point, it's very tempting to go back to what you know and who you've been. This is a moment of darkness where we are asked to acknowledge where we are and to keep walking forward through the dark. For me, this has shown up most in my marriage.

I had to leave the familiar and embrace the unknown to get to the real type of safety that I actually desired. I had to abandon the false sense of safety and step into the unknown to discover true safety. Leaving the familiar is like getting out of your cozy and warm bed in the middle of the night in the winter to go to the bathroom outside, getting caught in a ferocious blizzard and stuck in a sticky, frigid mud.

The truth is that I was always running away from the fact that I never felt safe with my dad, or within myself. I was seeking what I didn't get with him with every other man. It's not that I didn't ever feel physically safe with my dad—because I did at times—but it would never last. Emotionally, I witnessed how much he judged and discarded parts of my mum that lived deep inside of me. So even if I did feel physically safe with him, energetically, there was always a part of me that I had to hide in order to hold onto that safety. Or at least that is what I believed, based on what I witnessed. I was always looking for something that he couldn't completely give me. And I needed to find it in someone else. The more that I relied on others for my safety, the more that I had to become someone that I wasn't in order to get what I wanted. The more I became my authentic self I felt less safe and seen with him. I grew up trying to be the woman whom I thought he wanted, and as I became older and realised who that was, the less I was able to be her.

If we believe that our source of safety (or anything) is outside of us, then we are ultimately always going to be dependent on that source. We will never be free or independent; we create a separation from ourselves. No one can make you feel safe for long. If they do, it will be temporary, because we can't be with that person forever. The universe is constantly showing us where our attachment is by challenging it and putting us in situations where it is threatened. Our triggers are the energetic signs that point us towards our healing. The best part is that we don't have to go out looking for them, we simply have to live. Our emotional wounds will continue to be poked at energetically until we start to heal them. So if we believe that we are unsafe, and that our safety is reliant on an outside source then our life will continue to bring forward experiences and people that will challenge that.

In high school, I obsessively jumped from boy to boy, searching for the ones I most wanted. Whenever I really wanted to be with someone, it would never happen, and if I was with someone who really wanted to be with me, I would drop them. If our sense of safety is attached to an external source, like money or a relationship, the universe is going to bring that forward. It is going to bring forward situations and experiences that will test this dependency we've created so that we can eventually recognise that our source cannot possibly be outside of ourselves.

As a society, especially in the West, we are scared of death. Most people don't think about death until they are forced to. We do our best to deny it, and when it happens, we still cover it up. We work so hard to prolong life. The anti-aging market is a billion dollar industry. When someone dies, instead of saying that they have died we often move towards easier and lighter phrases like "they passed" or "they have passed on." Once death is here, we embalm the body and dress the person up as if they were still alive. Often, makeup and bright colours are used to create an image of happiness, health, and life. We bury them with their things, denying the fact that it will sit there permanently with a decomposing body. From the moment someone dies, we hide their body, discarding it to the people and businesses who specifically deal with "death." Once someone or something dies, we resist talking about them as if they are no longer here. We fear the dark side of life. We fear what night brings, and if we can't be in control in every moment, we are left with the complexities and challenges of our perceived inadequacies. We are left with fears of the unknown. We are left with the truth of who we are. We all know that when we experience death in our life, we much prefer to be with someone who welcomes death and is okay in the dark rather than someone who fears it. Grief is such a wild emotion, and it isn't something that can be fixed or softened. When we are in the dark, we want to be with someone who enjoys darkness and can be there in the stillness. We want to be with someone who has embraced their inner wild self and isn't hiding from their own darkness. Whenever I see a dead animal on the road, I always used to get upset and turn away from it to shield myself from the tragedy of its death. Overtime, this response felt less and less authentic. I began to wonder what I was trying to protect myself from. As I began to explore this inside, I noticed a desire to sometimes pull over, if I was alone, and move the animal off the road. Instead of hiding from its death, I turned towards it and began to honour it. Sometimes this is really uncomfortable, when there's a lot of blood and the body has already been quite deformed from its time on the road. Sometimes I encircle its body with stones, twigs and even flowers which I gather from the roadside. Sometimes it's impossible to move it. In those moments, I sit with its body and send some prayers to mother nature and the animal gods to support its soul in the transition. I find that it's always different, and it's really about whether I'm willing to sit with the animal in its death rather than turn away from it.

Part of the reason why I feel so safe with animals is because I have always felt like I know them. Animals don't hide who they are, or do things to manipulate or control your love for them. They are who they are, and their love for you is unconditional. I have always found it interesting how we can be so naked with animals without noticing it. When our dogs follow us into the bathroom, we don't wonder what they think of us. We embrace them being there with us in our most vulnerable moments.

I wasn't there when my horse Mac died, but I knew something had happened. The herd surrounded him as he lay in the grass in the middle of the back pasture at the ranch. They surrounded him in a circle, wither to wither, as if they were in ceremony. They were protecting his body from any scavengers, and they stood there until morning when the wrangler arrived. One by one, they left the circle. Even though I wasn't able to be there for him and witness this magic, I felt it. I woke up in the middle of the night in a panic, sweating and feverish. Mac and I were deeply connected, and for many years, he was the reason I kept myself alive. I felt safe on his back. We were soul mates, and he still stands by me as one of my animal guides. I always feel him on my right shoulder, supporting me. Animals remind us of the paths we have walked and the paths that we have chosen to walk, because they are so present with life. By being their authentic selves, they invite us into that space, and that is a place where our inner exploration is infinite. I love witnessing animal spirits because they are who they were in the physical world, following us around, playing, and sitting on our laps or at the foot of our bed. They continue to love, guide, guard, and protect us.

There is no real safety in life. We are all going to die, and there is no "right" time to die. Death is just as important as life is. Just as dark is necessary for light. Everything that we perceive as a threat to our safety is showing us our fear of death. No matter how hard we try, it is impossible to completely safety-proof our lives. The almost invisible line between life and death is one that we don't control. When we are grounded in ourselves and our connection with the divine, we are safe. When we live in union with the dark and the light, we are safe. When we believe that one is better than the other, we are not safe.

When do you feel most safe?

What threatens your idea of safety?

Did you grow up feeling safe?

Do you see someone or something as your source of safety?

Do you feel safe when you are alone with yourself?

Do you feel more safe in the light than the dark?

What is it about darkness that makes you feel unsafe?

"When you do things from your soul,
you feel a river moving in you, a joy."

- RUMI

CHAPTER 15

THE KNIGHT

"The most dangerous woman of all is the one who refuses to rely on your sword to save her because she carries her own."

- R.H. SIN

"This is what you do every single time, Chloe. You work yourself up and get caught in fear. This is your pattern. Here's what happens: first, you receive an idea for a new offering. You create it seemingly spontaneously. It emerges quickly, without much effort, and you release it out into the world with relative ease. People get excited and start signing up. In the beginning, it's great, and then something happens. You can't quite put a pulse on it, but you feel dissatisfied with what you're creating. And then it comes time for the preparation. This is when you really start creating chaos. The closer the start of the event is, the louder your mind gets and you essentially jump off the path. You try to get out of it, contemplate cancelling and refunding everyone. You think of escape routes and exit paths. Anything to run away and hide. In these moments, this is where I come in. I find myself wanting to ground you into your intuition and connect you back to the present moment. It's a lot of reminding you how many times this has happened before and reflecting back to you the end result. Telling you what you've told me in the past. Getting you out of the seriousness and into laughter when I can. And then you go on a nice bender where I kind of have you and kind of don't. And then there is a 48-hour window before the event where you get into a new state of doubt where it becomes slightly silly. Almost like you inhaled helium, which is okay. I see my job as helping you to maintain the silliness and keep you away from something more toxic. On the day of, I get out of your way. At this point, you're ready and it's up to you. I give you that space and see who I know: a powerful witch." Faris took a deep breath in and placed his hand on mine. My head was in between my legs, hanging in between a state of laughter and crying. This wasn't the first time Faris held this type of space for me, but when it happened, I really needed it. In those moments, it was like he saw something that I couldn't and held that vision up for me until I was ready to acknowledge it. Before

I met Faris, I hid these parts of myself from most people, especially partners. I tested it in some moments, like a young wolf pup peeking its head out of the cave to check for danger, but I was never met with this type of love and understanding. So I stayed hidden.

I used to think that my worth relied on men's love and desire for me. Before I began to really witness my magic and the magic around me, this limiting belief remained true. I believed the patriarchal fairytale that I needed to be saved by a man. This diminishing belief was so deeply woven into my consciousness, that it was all that I looked for. Whenever I felt stuck, I prayed for a man. Whenever I felt lost or empty, I waited and sometimes reached out for a man to satiate me. There were so many moments when I would push a man away, and then sit in pain hoping that he would make some heroic gesture to win me back like they so often do in the movies. This never happened when I wanted it to, and in this cycle, I remained in the darkness of not knowing myself and never truly feeling satisfied.

I met my husband Faris on a night when we both weren't looking for each other. I was in Dubai visiting my dad for a few months, and Faris came as a plus one with our mutual friend to my dad's rugby sevens party.

I was walking alone in the dark along the side of the randomly lit street near my dad's friends house. I felt the hot desert stones dig into my bare feet. I carried my black strappy high heels in my left hand, hanging down beside my barely there pleather skirt. I raised my hand to my eyes as a car's headlights pointed right at me. Expecting the silver Audi to drive by, it took me a couple of seconds to see that the car was actually coming to a stop. Faris and our mutual friend hopped out and I welcomed them to the party with a tray of freshly poured cocktails that I grabbed at the entrance. According to Faris' memory of this moment, time froze and he saw an aura of bright light around me, which at the time was both shocking and extremely unexpected for him, considering he didn't even know what an aura was. He recounts feeling that he had just met his future wife. As we walked towards the pool, drinks in hand, my dad entered the circle and randomly picked Faris up in excitement. This wasn't completely out of character for my dad, especially when he was drunk, but it was strange considering he had never met Faris before. Faris only stayed for a few hours, but when he left, he left with my number knowing that he had to see me again. The next day, he invited me to a house party with his friends, and thereafter, he continued to court me up until the moment that I had to return to Vancouver, a month after meeting. During that month, he managed to convince me to take him to Malaysia for a long weekend.

Faris in arabic translates to "knight." When we met, I was exorcising the part of me that craved a man for comfort. I had run away from my life in Canada to be with my dad and found what I thought I needed in him and his life. This meant a lot of drinking, schmoozing, partying, hosting, and pretending. At that time of my life, I was in the business of mostly ignoring my intuition and going to extremes in the hopes of getting what I wanted.

At that moment, when the Audi stopped, little did I know I was meeting my partner. I later learned the man driving the car, Faris, was a visionary. He's quirkishly stylish, gregarious by nature, and shockingly inventive. He never meets a stranger, a quality that reminded me of my dad.

On the surface, Faris was the perfect match for my wounded self. He was pushy, dominant, and controlling. The first time I noticed it, we were out for breakfast at my favourite french vegan cafe. When it came time for the bill, he shot his arm up into the air, calling out to the server with an aggression in his voice that was unmistakable. My stomach tightened and my eyes searched for the ground, alarmed by what I was witnessing in this cafe that I frequented daily. I continued to notice this behaviour, especially with customer service, and although I was mostly ashamed, there was a part of me that felt intrigued.

Faris was persistent. I wasn't sure how I felt, but something in me felt as though we had met before. The night after we met, I turned to him as we were leaving the bar and grabbed his arm. I said, "I feel like I know you." There was something about him that hooked me. Little did I know that he would become my husband, and we would live this big life together.

Before Faris, no romantic partner ever held his own with me. He challenged me in ways that I didn't think were possible, and he certainly made things alarmingly complicated at times, but ultimately, I've never had a teammate like Faris. I never had a partner who really showed up and sat with me in the times when I couldn't sit with myself. While we were living in Dubai we built an unhealthy pattern of communication where I would get stuck in what I was feeling, not communicate it, and ultimately have a painful row about it. Previous partners would melt or burn in my fire, but Faris stood his ground and even fought back with his own fire. What began to stand out to me was that after the argument, once we had both cooled down, Faris would sit with me as I processed and expressed what was going on. Sometimes it would be hours of listening and sharing. This was something I had never experienced before with a partner. It was a new level of vulnerability.

He took me to the cliffs of Cappadocia to propose to me, and we celebrated our engagement on the coast of Portugal in a manual RV that we both couldn't drive. That trip felt a bit more like a National Lampoons vacation than an engagement trip, but we made it out alive. The RV survived with just a few bumps and bruises. No man has taken the time to know me like Faris has. No partner has held the space for my emotions and big expressions like Faris does. My friend and mentor

Lynnette says, "It takes a courageous man to partner himself with a powerful witch," and I agree.

The first few years of our relationship was a fast and furious mix of honeymoon phase, shadow dancing, and feeling an unexplainable sense of being home. It wasn't until we left Dubai and moved back to North America that we were able to really see our destructive patterns and behaviours with each other. Faced with new issues around money, our jobs, and where we would live, it became increasingly difficult to feel safe and grounded together. Our fights were explosive and damaging, especially when alcohol was involved. One night when we were in London, our fight became physical, and I woke up in the morning ready to die from inescapable shame. Seeing the effects of our fight all over Faris's face and body was both a loud wake up call and a very good reason to dive into a pool of darkness. We hit rock bottom. Our fights began to remind me of the fights that I watched as a kid between my parents.

One night in Dubai, my inner fire and self-sabotage caused him to lose control of his emotions. This was one of the first times I really saw the damage I was doing to myself. Because of this, and what I grew up around, I would unleash my darkness in the way that I learned and witnessed in my mum. The feelings that I felt were uncontrollable, and they needed to be spewed out into the world or onto someone. They would come out in a desperate rage—a fire that would only grow if anything was in its path. On this night, Faris was in its path. We had yet to do any conscious work together, so not only was I deep in my unconscious coping, but so was Faris. In these moments, when he witnessed my shadow, he would respond with judgment and disgust. How could he love this part of me? Given his cultural and ancestral background, the only way forward for him was to control me, to shut me down and say the things that he needed to say to disengage my fire. To love this part of me, he would need to love this part of him, too—something that he couldn't comprehend at the time. As my rage continued to splatter around the apartment, his fear of me widened. In these moments, the truth is that I knew where I was going and how far I could go. I was well rehearsed with this scene. Not only had I seen it many times in my parents, but I also had a lot of practice in my own life. I had taken myself to the ultimate extreme point where another step forward would be a step too far, the point of no return. Instead of sharing the pain that I felt, I painted it all over our apartment in a tantrum, using our furniture and my body as the canvas. I ripped my shirt, pulled my hair, and banged my body against the walls. If Faris showed any offense, I would simply increase the volume of my force. At this point, I wanted to inflict pain. Pain was the only solution to how I was feeling. Nothing else made sense. My internal rage was abruptly severed by an unfamiliar response. Faris's entire demeanor shifted instantaneously from an angry, dominant man to a soft, vulnerable child. Suddenly a little boy sat in front of me, huffing and puffing in efforts to grab onto some air. My mood shifted up the emotional scale in a drastic emergency response. He couldn't take this. I had hurt him by losing touch with myself and falling into the darkness. I sat with him, uncomfortably brushing his shoulder and encouraging him to take deep breaths. A part of me felt angry; another part was terrified and unfamiliarly vulnerable. This wasn't the first time that I felt like my emotions were too much for someone, but this was certainly the first time I saw the direct impact on someone else.

This was one of the first times that I felt the remorse and guilt of my destruction. Amidst my temper tantrum, I caused the person whom I loved the most to experience intense fear and panic. It was like looking into a mirror, except the person on the other side was Faris, my husband. In that moment, and moments after, I saw my inner child and the trauma that she dealt with growing up. The panic that Faris felt was the same panic that I felt witnessing my parents' fight and my mum live through her rage and terror. My brother and I were always there in the house or in the middle, absorbing all of the energy like black sponges. That night, I felt struck by lightning and my internal dialogue began to shift. I started to notice the effect that words have and the power that they carry. Words are not just words; they are energetic beings, and from the moment they leave our lips, they become their own living creature. They interact with the world and engage with those who are in their presence. They are felt. They are energy.

A few months later after planting a few seeds and waiting, Faris agreed to join me in an intuitive session with Dr. Divi. The day of, my mind created every possible scenario not to go. Clearly, there was something I was hiding from. We walked in as strangers, and during the session, we were asked to surrender. We both felt hurt by the truths that were shared and what connected us was our fear of the future. Faris was angry with me for seeing my dad's flaws in him, and unknowingly projecting his stories about his mum onto me. He felt controlled by me. I was angry at him for mirroring my childhood back to me where I felt alone, unseen, and dishonoured. With another person in the room, a referee, we had to respect each other. We were asked not to speak over one another, cut each other off, or edit what was shared. This was the most vulnerable I had ever been with a partner. When we walked out of the room, we each had a call to action, and the path forward was unknown. We couldn't take back what was said. We were still together, but a large part of who we had been was being released, and in its place was empty space. We were in the dark without the safe illusion of not knowing each other's deepest hidden truths.

Faris left on a business trip for three weeks the day after that session, and we didn't see each again until the Christmas holidays in Mexico with my family. I arrived in Mexico a few days after Faris, and the moment we saw each other I felt awkward and uncomfortable. I didn't want him to touch me, and we felt more like strangers than partners. I tried to maintain a sense of peace and civility, but I couldn't hide the fact that I was completely shut off from any sexual connection or intimacy. Every time Faris reached out to grab my hand or put his hands around my waist, I shuddered and pulled away. My body and heart were shut off, and I didn't know how to shift it. When I saw Faris, I realised that I had spent the past 4 weeks building a powerful story against him and disconnecting myself from him. Out of desperation, Faris asked me to join him for a drink without the family. The moment he mentioned sex my body cringed. I began to realise that from this place of feeling unsafe, unloved, and unprotected, my body had built a wall between us. In telling each other our darkest truths and fears in that session with Dr. Divi and not having time to process it together, an impenetrable wall was constructed subconsciously.

During this time of darkness, sex complicated everything. As long as I continued to feel like I wasn't safe, supported, or respected by Faris, having sex with him felt like a self betrayal. It felt like a continuation of my entire history with men, sabotaging and sacrificing myself in order to feel loved and wanted. As with my experience with intuition, I got to a point where I couldn't ignore my feelings anymore. I couldn't have sex with Faris anymore. I couldn't risk having children in a relationship that felt all too similar to my parents'. I needed to heal and we needed to heal together. I was willing to face the fear that withholding my body would equate to him leaving or looking for pleasure and connection somewhere else with someone else. I could no longer live in the cycle of thinking about having sex and then checking it off of a list as if it were a household chore I was completing. Knowing deep down that it was really a safety checklist to remain safe in my relationship. I could no longer push down my feelings for a temporary fix. When we are intimate with someone that we don't want to be intimate with or don't feel safe with, we send our body a message. On some level, an inauthentic intimate experience creates trauma in the body. In order to participate, you must shut off a part of you. When we shut off connection and feeling, we shut off our intuition. I had a lot of sex in my life, but I had never had sex consciously with my heart and soul open. And so we stopped having sex, and Faris agreed to give me space without a timeline, knowing that this journey inwards could lead us to separating.

Faris didn't leave me and he didn't cheat on me, despite my belief that he would. I didn't leave him or cheat on him, despite my previous track record of fleeing and destroying. The unconditional love and understanding that Faris brought into our relationship caught me off guard. Despite our flaws and destructive habits, he stayed and walked through the flames of discomfort with me. He gave me the space to explore myself, without the pressures of sex and intimacy, and this allowed me to really deeply heal. By stepping into his divine masculine, he became my fierce protector and partner without needing me to be saved by him. Instead of forcing his needs onto me, he took a step back and supported me to find true intimacy with myself first. By encouraging me to listen to and follow my intuition, he allowed himself to do the same, and so during this time we both grew and healed. Faris joined a conscious men's group, and he worked with a coach with the pieces that were coming up for him. We stopped having sex for many months, and we worked through all of the limiting stories that came up together.

I had to let go of my expectations that Faris (or another man) would save me, so that I could allow Faris to be my knight. I had to kill the part of me that wanted to be saved, and with it, my attachment to all of the stories and memories that bred that belief. Our relationship has provided the vessel for me to begin exploring the truth of who I am, moving along the unpaved, thorny, dark pathway. As our relationship

"We must be willing to let go of the life we have planned, so as to have the life that is waiting for us."

- E. M. FORSTER

has progressed, I have continued to come to the same truth: I am building something that I have no real proof of existence, and I am building from no model of reference. This is the unknown, and when we walk in the unknown, we are forced to trust our intuition because we have no frame of reference or map to guide us. We must listen.

I had to embrace my "dark emotions" of shame, anger, jealousy, and resentment and learn how to be with them. This is something that I had no proof or evidence of in my life. No one else around me expressed these dark emotions in a healthy way. They were always shown to me in toxic ways: emotional abuse, fighting, or projections. It's easy to love someone when they are in their light. Our world supports joy, happiness, love, and excitement. When my emotions embodied a calm and peaceful ocean, I received a lot of praise. When my emotions represented an angry, disturbed, and unpredictable ocean, I received judgment and shame. When Faris and I started dating, something he would often say was that he didn't love my shadow self. At the time, this was accurate because he was a reflection of me. I hated my shadow self. I judged her and shamed her, and when she appeared, it took me days to find my way back to normal. She was forbidden and exiled from my life. She made me look weak, out of control, and ugly. I did my best to show everyone a person who was beautiful and easy to love, and she would appear to tear it all down. She was powerful and I hated her. And I hated Faris's shadow too. I had no space for him, and when he showed up, I shamed him. We shadow danced for quite some time, pushing each other's buttons, fighting, and hurting each other. Our relationship with each other was similar to my relationship with myself. A section of beautiful, fun, light days followed by the sudden onslaught of darkness that tore us apart and dismantled the illusion of unconditional love. This was my work and this was our work. We each had to learn how to love each other's vulnerabilities and recognise that our relationship was less about the surface stuff and more about the deep, internal, spiritual growth that was happening behind the scenes.

Growing up, I always played the scenario in my head that my boyfriend or my dad (or any man, for that matter) would decide to turn against the current and come back to me. I would sit in my pain, in the dark, waiting for their call or their arrival, waiting for the romantic or heroic act that I had been promised. I waited for that moment when a lightbulb goes off in a man's head and he races against odds to confess his love or save the woman from her doom, or herself. I waited, and waited, and because of my extreme attachment to this unsavoury expectation, I continued to feel disappointed. The story was that without a man to rescue me, I would ultimately never be truly happy. An unrealistic narrative that many women look for and men either run towards or away from.

In wolf packs, the female wolves fight to the death. For the females, it is a matter of survival, so if they have mated and had pups they will fight to kill. Rarely will you see a male dog pick a fight with a female for that exact reason. The race to being alpha female in the pack is a brutal competition for the right to pass on one's genes. The males are comparatively laid back, establishing their status in the hierarchy through threats and less serious actions. The females draw blood.

In a herd of horses, the leader of the herd is usually the oldest mare. The male horse (there are usually one to two geldings in a herd) still holds leadership of the herd but is seen more as the protector than the leader. The lead mare might be physically weaker, but she has the most experience, having survived the most threats. She commands the other horses to obey and respect her. Elephants herds are also matriarchal, led by the oldest and most experienced female elephant.

For me, there is nothing more terrifying than a mother because she has nothing to lose when it comes to protecting her young. A mother's love is fierce like no other. So why have we come to believe, as women, that we need saving? When in nature, we are seen as the leaders and the ones to fear the most. Even though my mum didn't always see it or feel it because of her own limiting fears and stories when she was forced into her power to protect us, there was nothing more frightening. It took me some time and maturity to really see it, but my mum showed incredible strength and tenacity in our childhood. Moving to new countries with completely new and extreme climates with young children away from all family and friends. In the rune family, the rune Berkana is known as the untamed mother rune. It embodies the qualities of the feminine: nurturing, creation, destruction, and protection. In nature, a mother animal is deeply connected to her maternal role and honours it unquestionably. Mother animals are also known to kill and eat their young if they are sick, injured, or weak. This is an innate behaviour to increase chances of survival of the rest of the litter as well as the mother herself. If you watch a female dog with her litter, it's clear that the role of the mother is not just to feed, clean, and love her pups. She also teaches them about the world outside of their den and the importance of boundaries and behaviour. To a human, it almost seems abusive sometimes as a mother growls fearlessly at her pups, and gradually increases the severity of her response if the pups keep pushing. We would perhaps use words like "savage" or "tragic" to describe these wild and very natural behaviours that we witness. The truth is that there is nothing savage about the irreverent nature of a mother. She is teaching them how to survive in ways that other members of the family either can't or won't. She is giving them invaluable tools, without which they could be abandoned or killed, especially in the wild. This topic always reminds me of Berkana and deepens my appreciation for the gifts of the mother role in nature. What I appreciate most about Berkana is the sharp duality of how a mother channels her love, depending on what is needed. A mother is both deeply nurturing, and she can also be unexpectedly lethal. In the wild, the mother will feed and protect her young, and she will also kill and even eat them, if necessary.

The Nordic gods, and gods in general, get their power from us relying on them. The hierarchical belief system is what keeps their power intact. Lynnette and I were discussing this, and I thought of the Northern mythological Giantess, Angrboda. As the story goes, I mentioned how she "lured" Loki into the forest. Lynnette immediately stopped me in my tracks, and challenged me to look at the word "lured" and if it's the truth. This is the story and perspective of Odin. Most of the rune stories are told by men. Even those of us who have done the work and feel empowered are still conditioned by the patriarchy. In Women Rose Rooted, Sharon Blackie writes, "The story of Eve in the Book of Genesis is the underpinning of countless measures which have limited the actions, rights, and status of women. No matter what women might achieve in the world, the fundamental message of the sacred texts of the world's largest religious grouping, which for 2,000 years have supplied foundational beliefs of our Western culture, is that men should not trust women, and that women should trust neither themselves nor each other." It's ironic that Angrboda would lure the original trickster, Loki. It is possible that Loki and Angrboda fell in love, and no one was lured. But that story is boring, and it fails to demonise Angrboda and her monstrous children, Fenrir the ferocious wolf, Hela the keeper of Hell and Jormungand, the death-eating serpent.

Since I was a little girl, my mum told me that I had the ability to lure men in and manipulate them with my eyes. She would tell me that this was how I gained control of them, and it made her feel inadequate because she believed she wasn't pretty or beautiful enough to do the same. The tragedy is that for quite some time I believed her and lived by that story. I let that story run me, which meant that my ego led the way when it came to men and attraction. This is a story that is told through the patriarchal perspective. This was a story my mum learned as a child, and it had the opposite effect on her, having her feel inadequate and never enough despite her incredible beauty and potent wisdom. Women are not here to lure men in or put them under a spell. It was Loki's choice to go into the forest and fall in love with Angrboda. Their love was beautiful and authentic. But not to Odin and the gods because they hated Angrboda and feared her power. They feared what she brought and might bring to their world.

Marianne Williamson's famous quote says, "Our deepest fear is not that we are inadequate. Our deepest fear is that we are powerful beyond measure. It is our light, not our darkness that most frightens us." In wolf packs, the alpha is the least vocal of the group. When it speaks, it speaks with power and others listen. It doesn't simply speak to fill space or get attention. It is always intentional with its movements. A woman in her power is just that. She doesn't need attention; she commands it by simply being herself. People are drawn to her for authenticity and her ability to stand with you in the light or dark. Perhaps women have been given these stories to believe that they are not enough without men because the truth is that we are more than enough. Perhaps we are told that we need to be saved by men because deep down, the truth is that we are powerful beyond belief. Having others in her life and sharing energies is about choice, not necessity.

I can't say for sure what kept us going in our marriage. It wasn't just one thing. It was a collection of many moments. I had to choose to look at myself differently, to step into the center of my life instead of simply following the energy of my thoughts and fears. We both had to hang up any stories and expectations of what a marriage should look like or be like. Those hidden rules and standards that suddenly show themselves when you are on the edge of your experience. Rules like how many times a week or month you "should" be having sex, or what not having sex means to the longevity of the relationship. Rules about what is good communication, what is bad, what red flags are, and what to do when they start flying. Intimacy is something that can't be replicated from one experience to the next; it is unique to each moment. Discovering, fostering, and nurturing intimacy with a long-term partner takes something. It is a reflection of the intimacy that we allow with ourselves.

I stood in the middle of my decision between staying and leaving my marriage for quite some time, contemplating my exit. My mind was collecting proof to justify my exit. Looking for things to back my fear up. It took a lot of digging and patience to get to the roots of what I was feeling and what I was fearing, to recognise that what I feared most was the level of love that Faris brought to our partnership. The type of love that I was taught to fear and see as a weapon. Something that would be used against me later in life, or even worse, taken from me. I knew that it would come to a choice, and that the choice was mine. I had to choose to leave or stay. It was a similar decision I was faced with that night at the ranch with my ancestors. Once again, I had to choose to open my heart and walk through the unknown and the fires of my fear.

If you were to tell your partner the most honest truth, what would it be?

What standards and stories do you hold over yourself and your relationship that keep you stuck?

How is your partner your mirror?

How are you hiding in your relationship?

What happens to you when someone loves you unconditionally?

What is your relationship with intimacy?

What happens when things get "hard," do you run or do you work through it?

CHAPTER 16

EXPOSED

"At some point in a woman's life,
she just gets tired of being ashamed all of the time.
After that, she is free to become whoever she truly is."
— ELIZABETH GILBERT

It's taken me time to learn how to hold my ground and speak my truth. And I am certainly not a perfect student of truth. When I was younger, I remember noticing how much my Dad fibbed—white lies here, white lies there. Lying became part of his reality, and as a result, it became a part of mine too. Most of them were harmless exaggerations but what I've learned is that with energy, everything creates something. It wasn't until I met Faris that I really began to tell someone all of my truth. When I was with my ex-boyfriend, Mark, I lied a lot. I hid what I feared he couldn't handle; I hid my feelings and I built a massive wall of shame that divided us. I couldn't do this with Faris. He was the first man who wouldn't allow it, not because he controlled me but because of his desire to listen. I wanted to tell him the truth. I wanted him to know me.

Once a word is spoken, it is no longer yours to control. It becomes its own essence. I once read that when we speak, we cast spells. A word is an energetic manifestation of what dwells inside, and when we tell lies, it is a representation of the lies that live within us. I was scared to use my voice. I was scared to be heard.

Conversations and interactions are not always meant to go smoothly and peacefully. Sometimes the wind blows silently, and other times the wind sings and wails moving from one direction to the next, catching your attention and creating destruction as it moves. It's difficult to speak your truth when you know that it isn't going to resonate with the person it needs to be shared with. Those are the fiery points of vulnerability where you are sitting on the edge of a balancing beam, one side representing a safe space of silence and the other side representing the unpredictable space of speaking up. How often do we actually speak up and share what is on our mind? How often do we actually set a boundary? I used to love the role of the chameleon, transforming my presentation and appearance based on my surroundings. It was a survival instinct I used to be unseen by potential predators. One of the issues with speaking my truth is that I have to back it up once it's been spoken. I can't release it out into the world and then walk away as if I haven't. Brené Brown called this the "vulnerability hangover." This is the moment after you've spoken a deep truth when you return to your mind and your logical self and you realise the impact of what you've done. Vulnerability is such an interesting state of being because it is always changing and the line of what is vulnerable is always moving based on our growth. The beauty in this is that once you walk an unmarked path, you know everything about it. You know how it feels, the shoes it requires, and how much water you need to bring with you. And sometimes it feels good to revisit it when you are in need of something comfortable and familiar, a reminder of your courage and abilities.

Over Christmas, my mum, brother, and sister-in-law, Tori, got into an argument. Faris and I were in Austin away from family because of travel restrictions, but we overheard different parts of the conflict from different perspectives. When Tori called me and told some of the things that she said to my mum, I felt triggered. In her anger, she told my mum to "fuck off." I felt protective of my mum and began to build a story of what that meant. I tried to bury my feelings and let it go, but co-existing in a family of intuitives and witches (Tori and my mum are both also intuitives) means that nothing stays hidden for long. Tori and I ended up getting into an argument, which resulted in a deeper more intimate conversation a day later to explore each other's perspectives and feelings. It was painful, confrontational, and uncomfortable. It was also vulnerable, mature, and deeply conscious. We went from two triggered, wounded women projecting onto each other to two deeply conscious women and sisters who loved each other and chose to hold space for each other's pain. It was like nothing I had ever experienced before. We were both using our voices in a way that women haven't. Instead of staying in our stories, we walked through fire, water, and air together to arrive in earth energy. Although a part of me already felt it, I had kept myself from acknowledging that in-law families are complicated, because I missed my mum and felt like Tori wasn't appreciating her presence. In conflict, it's easier to stay in your story and fuel your fire rather than to step outside of it and see how we both hold something that could help one another. So often, conflicts like these create major boulders in relationships, and if left alone to fester for too long, they create huge divides in families that can last generations. When you look at families and marriage from a soul perspective, there is always something that our in-laws are bringing forward for us. It doesn't always make it easier to know that, but it provides a bridge for us to walk over and be tender with ourselves as we navigate the storms of miscommunication. Something that this opportunity reminded me of is that we all come from different experiences and so what is normal for me might not be normal for you. That being said, in every expression of reality, there is something at the core that connects us. It is available to us, if we are willing to sit with it and call it forward. With Tori, we've been close since the moment my brother introduced us, and I'm grateful to have her in our family. She brings even more of that "wild" essence that I crave and call out for, and sometimes when wild women gather, the fire burns brightly.

The first time I consciously witnessed authentic power in a woman was during a writing retreat that I attended with my mum. The retreat was hosted by the dynamic duo in the writing world, Elizabeth Gilbert and Cheryl Strayed. They had decided to combine forces based on the successes of their books, Big Magic and Brave Enough. The workshop was subsequently called, Brave Magic. It was the end of the weekend, and Elizabeth and Cheryl were opening up the space for an intimate group Q&A, which came along with some clear instructions about what was a question and what wasn't a question. Although she didn't mention it, it was clear that Elizabeth was practicing boundaries and protecting her loved ones after having been in the public eye a bit too much as of late. It was one of those situations where what happened next was so clearly meant to happen, to create some form of learning. The air was thick with spiritual messages as if this was a moment for women to heal something greater in our lineages together. As Elizabeth shared her "guidelines," you could feel the tension in the room. The first lady that was picked on to ask a question raised her body from her chair, parted her lips, and began with, "Sooo, I know you just said to not do this, but I am going to choose to be really brave and..." "Excuse me, sit down!" Elizabeth Gilbert declared with an untamed command, towering over Cheryl who sat beside her. The woman's voice was cut off by the sharp reiteration of Elizabeth's truth. A clear impenetrable boundary had been set. This was one of her first public events since releasing so much of her own personal life and changes with the world on social media, including the fact that she was in love with her best friend; a woman, who was currently battling cancer. The reverberant sound in the room spoke louder than the words themselves. There was a palpable divide between people who were for boundaries and people who weren't. Some people whispered under their breath that they thought Liz was being harsh and unfair, while other people commended her for standing her ground and speaking up. This was one of the first times I had witnessed a woman hold her center in this way. This was the first time that I witnessed a woman follow her instinct, despite knowing that others might reject her for it. This moment was permanently locked into my brain, filed under "role models" and I always reflect back on it in moments when I am wavering on an intuitive choice because of a fear of being disliked.

The thing I always find I ask myself and other women is whether we actually say what we feel. Do you tell the truth, or do you conceal it and say something "nicer" to soften the blow or to keep things calm? We don't want to hurt someone's feelings or disappoint them, or be rejected ourselves so we withhold. We withhold our feelings, and we shut our throats. We are so conditioned to hide the truth and soften it with light. We are a muted society. In today's world, we are noticing just how much truth is hidden from us on every single level.

The year 2020 revealed deep and dark truths. Truths that have been existing for many years are only just beginning to come out. It is impossible to stay silenced forever. Truth is an energy that will find its own path if we don't support its movement. Energy will never stay still and stagnant forever. It cannot be stopped. Censorship is a major issue that we are noticing on all platforms and especially in the media, and it is important for us to look at what our external reality is showing us about what's going on inside. Whether we are protecting ourselves or another person, we are doing no one a service by withholding the truth and denying our intuitive guidance. I've heard stories where counsellors who are supervising new grads in their work will lightly recommend for them to take antidepressants as a way to manage the anxiety and energy that they feel as they begin working with people. How can we expect to be in service, connect to others, and help if we are shutting off our internal messaging systems? We all have innate wisdom within us and the tools to guide ourselves along the path, and we have been trained and taught to shut it all down and close it all off to rely on external sources to give us healing, answers, and solutions. To fix us. The remedy to our wholeness is within our divine self and learning to fully embrace and express all of who we are. We are scared of our darkness. We are scared of the power of our darkness. And our fear breeds uncontrollable darkness.

One morning, soon after moving into our new house in Austin, I was having coffee with my friend Jamie and sharing stories. I call Jamie "Tarzan baby" because she reminds me of a wild jungle child. She has a certain fire about her that invokes the inner child in me. Her big, beautiful, piercing blue eyes, messy freckles, and bouncy wild hair always make me feel like we're swinging on branches in the jungle when we're together. On this day, we were talking about the roots of our experiences and how our relationships are the expressions of our wounds from the past. She and I have similar relationship wounds, so it's always a breath of fresh air to hear that she is working through them as I am. The unfortunate truth is that oftentimes our romantic relationships are expressions of our family of origin wounds. Jamie was recognising that she gets anxious in relationships when the men don't show up as she expects them to. What we began to reveal in our sharing was that the anxiety was oftentimes a sign that she wasn't speaking her truth or listening to her intuition. She was looking for something inside of the men that she wasn't going to find or that wouldn't satisfy her. And the moment that they let her down or disrespected her, she would get angry and shut down instead of telling them the truth. For whatever reason, she believed that telling men the truth would create an unwelcome and unwanted outcome. So she shut herself away into a metaphorical cave, only to come out once the invoked feelings were gone. Underneath it all, a part of her expected the men to come and save her or to read between the lines and show up as she wanted them to. This never happens, and so she continues to repeat the pattern never really letting them get close enough to her to really share that space of vulnerable intimacy.

I did this too. For too long. I was running off of a wound that was left to fester over time.

It took me many years to come to terms with who my parents were and release the need for them to be someone that they weren't. The thing about relationships is that most of the time people show us who they are. We just choose not to see it, or we choose to see it through rose-coloured glasses because we don't want to accept the truth. We want to change them, impact them, or believe in something different, something easier. So we stay where we are and continue to deepen the wound of feeling resentful and angry. We continue to weave together the tale that is as old as time.

Intimacy is not easy. True intimacy requires vulnerability from both sides. In order to be vulnerable, we need to feel safe and we need to feel seen. We need to be willing to be seen. Intimacy begins in our relationship with ourselves when we are willing to tell ourselves the truth and be with whatever it is that comes up within us. We are most vulnerable in those intimate moments when the production lights and masks are stripped away and we are being in the expression of whatever we are, the messy moments. The moments we are usually sitting with or in some darkness. Vulnerability and darkness come together; they are partners.

Connecting with our intuition requires intimacy. As we are poked and prodded by life, our mind tries its best to distract us from the truth by holding onto old stories and thoughts that keep us safe. In my relationship with Faris, it was much easier to focus on what he was doing wrong and who he wasn't being rather than to look at how I was protecting myself. Whenever we would fight or have a disagreement, my mind would cleverly dip into my pool of past stories to bring forward whatever thought would best fit the scenario. It's always easier to focus on the present moment or relationship that has less charge to it, than the root cause or wound from childhood. It's easier to stay on the surface where it's lighter, than to dive under the surface, into the roots where it's darker, and harder to breathe. Instead of seeing that Faris was showing me my beliefs about men and safety, I stayed on the surface where the anger was strongest and the energy of blame was most available. I stayed here on this cyclical track until I started working with Lynnette and allowed her into my inner realms. As I began to dive deeper into myself and allow another human being inside with me, my comfort and familiarity with intimacy and trust shifted.

Being the messenger of truth isn't always a glamorous job. It can mean many things, including being deeply disliked. It can mean judgment and fear. It can mean isolation. I think this is part of the reason why so many people have dishonoured their truth for so long. Telling the truth and being a stand for truth means you will likely be disliked by others. There is no negotiation on that. Not everyone is ready to hear the truth or to stand in their truth. In so many ways, we have been conditioned to believe lies and to hold back our truth so that we can stay alive. During the historical witch trials, other women sacrificed their friends and sisters for survival, oftentimes telling lies to keep themselves safe. In each of us, we carry the memory of being killed, burned, and hung for telling the truth. We all hold a not so distant memory of punishment and trauma for listening to, and following, our intuition. And we also carry the memory of lying to ourselves and each other. For so many years, it has been conditioned and pushed out of us to create space for more brainwashing, control, and fear. For so long, the women who stood out of the crowd, told a different story, and looked differently have been ostracized and criticised. In some cases, they have even been killed.

How would you have responded if you were in the room with Elizabeth Gilbert when she stood her ground?

How do you respond when a woman shows her strength?

Are you a people pleaser?

Do you stand your ground?

Do you stay in your center?

What inspires/drives you in your life?

CHAPTER 17

LIFE FORCE

"Darkness is alive and its life is obscured by light.
Darkness puts out its tentacles and touches your face;
darkness licks at your eyes and grants you a different kind of sight."
- SHARON BLACKIE

That first year that I started working as a psychic full-time felt like a wild tornado. Within weeks of jumping on the spiritual bandwagon, a woman approached me who immediately felt like family. She emailed me, mentioning that her guides had led her to me and she felt we were meant to do some work together. I decided to call her without thinking about it. She picked up the phone and responded in a very proper British accent that reminded me of my Windsor family. We hit it off and within a few weeks, and we were hosting our first psychic dinner series together. Filled with incredibly indulgent holistic food, we also did individual and table readings for the guests, as they enjoyed the enchanting evening. This was the first time I did table readings, and one of the first times I ever did psychic readings in person. It happened so quickly that I had no time to question it or feed my fear. We called it The Witchery series, inspired by the actual Witchery, an old hotel and landmark in Edinburgh at the gates of the Castle. I had visited The Witchery during a trip to Scotland the previous Christmas with Faris. This haunting place that got its name from the hundreds of women and men who were burnt at the stake on Castlehill. We decided to have dinner there and I can barely remember the entire meal. It was almost as if I left my body and didn't return to it until we had left the eerie building. Our dinner series in Vancouver became popular very quickly, selling-out every event, and we decided to host a much bigger Witchery event for Samhain that year. We ended up selling 200 tickets, and rented an old building called Heritage Hall to host the event. We also co-hosted a psychic medium retreat for a group of 12 women just one week before. During the retreat, I felt bombarded by spirit energy. The entire long weekend, I felt like I was being followed and I wasn't clear on what it felt like to really stand in my center yet. I barely slept every night; it was as if the house was spiritually active at all hours and every spirit was coming to talk to me. That was the year when my excitement took over and I said "yes" to a lot of things. I was also straddling the fence, with one part of me holding onto my safe identity as a Holistic Nutritionist, and the old Chloe, while the other part of me was running in the direction of my new unknown life as a psychic. When I returned home from the Witchery dinner on Samhain night, I crashed. But I still wasn't done. I already agreed to some other big commitments, including another retreat, and even though I felt like I had nothing left, I kept going. A few months later, one rainy night I was crossing the street from the train station, and a car drove right into me. Up until this point, I had been getting a lot of messages and guidance to slow down and release some commitments from my schedule, but I ignored that guidance until it literally hit me. I was forced to slow down. Even though I didn't have any major injuries, I was really emotionally impacted by the accident, and my body was achy and sore for a few weeks. I had to shut everything down for at least a week, and face all of the parts of me that came up as I slowed down. It was time to slow down and do the inner work to find my center, my confidence, and learn how to work sustainably as a psychic. I needed to learn how to be in my power.

Working with the spirit world requires unmistakable boundaries and truth. Too often, intuitives leave their work because of burnout. It's really easy to become drained, especially if you are empathic and sensitive. Bypassing my truth, wanting to be liked, and avoiding disappointment are all fast-track highways to spiritual prostitution, and I took all of them. If you are a pushover, or you show signs of being lenient with your time and space, you will quickly lose yourself. There's such an invisible fine line between being kind and caring and being codependent. An invaluable lesson that all elders have taught me is how to stand my ground and be in my center, no matter what. You don't work as an intuitive to be popular and liked. You also don't work with spirit as a form of entertainment. The people that use energy work as entertainment are the ones who usually end up leaving their work. The people that see their work as their source are the ones who usually crash and burn. Not too many generations ago, we held beautiful and honourable connections to the land and to our ancestors. Every summer when we would visit our grandparents in England, I was always so floored that the milkman brought glass bottles of milk to their house straight from the dairy, and that a lot of the produce came straight from my grandpa's garden. Sometimes our life in Malaysia seemed more glamorous, but now I sometimes see that our expat life was actually just more complicated, and was missing the simplicity and the roots of ancestral connection. The roots taught us and kept us solid, especially when it came to working with spirit and magic. In the Celtic shamanic traditions, it is known that spirit work is sacred and commands respect and boundaries. As with all life, everything exists in the spirit world and like-attracts-like. If you enter the spirit world with dishonour and without boundaries, you are likely to attract those types of energies into your space. Just like in the human world. In essence, the spirit world works with us, supporting us in using our voices and holding our ground. They show us where our weaknesses are, and what we need to work on.

It really took something to get my green card. It was almost as if it was being delayed so I could work through everything that came up around my marriage with Faris and our commitment to each other. There were quite a few barriers in the way of my moving to America, including my parents' deeply inherited and ingrained abhorrence for the country. Pretty remarkably, the week after Faris and I did our first session with Dr. Divi where we told each other our unfiltered truths, I received the long awaited email that my U.S. Citizen interview was scheduled. It was in exactly a month and it was happening in Montreal. I decided to invite my mum and make a mother-daughter trip out of it.

The day of our flight, the east coast experienced one of the worst winter storms in a few decades. All of the airports closed and all flights were cancelled for a week. We ended up taking one of the most dangerous uber rides of our life from Toronto airport to downtown Toronto and caught the train from Toronto to Montreal.

We arrived in Montreal in the early evening, the day before my morning interview. One of the perks of being in Montreal was feeling like we were on holiday in Europe. I had booked the sweetest apartment in an old, renovated brick building with a big beautiful fireplace. The moment we walked up the black iron staircase and opened the front door, I felt an icy draft of energy run through my body, and it wasn't connected to the freezing temperatures outside. Despite how cute the apartment was, something about it felt off. I dropped my bags and clunky winter jacket to the floor and began my standard energy sweep. My mum called out to me to see something in one of the bedrooms, but my feet kept walking towards the back of the apartment near the kitchen. Something was pulling me towards this door at the very back like a magnet. The moment my hand touched the door knob, frosty shivers ran up and down my spine. It was a dark, small room with a twin bed and an old rickety closet with some suitcases stashed alongside the walls. Clearly, this was a makeshift room that was also used as storage, but there was something else I noticed. There in the dark corner of the room a child spirit was sitting on the floor staring at me. I slowly walked backwards, closed the door, and ran my hand around the corners of the door as if to reseal what I had just opened. I decided not to tell my mum and worry her. I needed to get my green card interview out of the way, and this wasn't the first time I felt or found spirits in a house.

I barely slept that night, but I attributed it to the fear of the interview that was just hours away. I happily passed the test (more what the interview felt like) of proving the validity of my marriage, and we spent the day shopping, exploring, and soaking in the wintery magic of Montreal. I completely forgot about the Airbnb and the boy in the back room. The next night, I was tormented all night long. Lights flickering on and off, doors opening and closing, images waking me up, temperatures rising and falling, and spirits jumping on top of me and touching me. I was so tired that I let it happen, trying my best to fall asleep and shut it all off. After a few hours, I woke up and joined my mum in her bedroom, hoping it would help. It didn't. It almost got worse. This was the first time that my mum really witnessed what I had been talking about since I was a little girl. I finally got up, turned the lights on, opened my mouth, and yelled, "IT IS TIME TO GO. YOU ARE NOT WELCOME HERE AND I AM NOT OPEN FOR BUSINESS." I lit the palo santo that I brought with me, put crystals around our bed, and held the energy of this boundary as if I was holding a sword on top of my sleeping body. I wasn't scared; I was pissed. We ended up sleeping for the rest of the night. The next morning after a few hours of sleep, I decided to do a mini clearing for the apartment. My mum and I opened all of the windows and doors, and I did a smoke clearing. I focused my energy on my bedroom, and the back room where the boy was. I asked him to go to the light and leave us alone. It was a tricky situation, because it wasn't my home, so I couldn't exactly banish the spirit or set clear boundaries. We ended up leaving that day, and I messaged the Airbnb owner letting him know that there was spiritual activity to be aware of and it could do with a good clearing. I never heard back from him.

    Moments like these have taught me how to use my voice, vocalise my boundaries, and hold my center. They've taught me how to transmute my fear. I used to be so scared to speak up and upset someone, even if it was a spirit that was taunting me. When I first started doing mediumship, I felt as though it was my duty to help every spirit that came to me. I had tethered myself to the identity of mediumship, and I had dropped all of my boundaries. When I saw this child in the dark corner of the room, part of me felt like I was responsible to help him. He was showing up in my space for a reason. This is a hard lesson to learn as an intuitive. Just because you can always help, doesn't mean you should. There is no such thing as a selfless helper, and if we give without consideration for ourselves, we quickly drain all of our energy. We drain our life force. Once you can help, it is important to set your boundaries around your work. If you make yourself endlessly available, everyone will try to use you—living or dead. Spirits need rules just as much as we do, especially because they can access us in many ways. If you allow them to, they will follow you around into all of your sacred spaces, asking for your help. If you don't acknowledge them, they might even demand it. Every teacher who I have worked with around spiritual communication has enforced the fact that you must be clear, stern, direct, and unwavering with the boundaries that you set. You can't leave room for questions, which is similar to working with animals. Animals communicate very clearly with each other and they never leave any grey area. It takes practice to hold that space because it isn't something that we do well with other humans. I used to be afraid to use my voice or to be seen as unreasonable or unhelpful. It reminded me of my mum when I was younger, and it took me some time to realise that those qualities in her were actually beautiful. They were maternal, lethal, and representative of the feminine fire. Recently, a volcano in Iceland called Fagradalsfjall, which has been dormant for 800 years, erupted. Watching its fire melt the mountain side into a glowing red and black river of lava reminded me of the feminine fire. When I see mother nature show her power in ways like this, it reminds me of the feminine fire that lives in every woman. The fire that so many of us hide. As a kid and teenager, I would do anything to avoid criticism or harsh feedback. I believed that others' experience of me reflected my worth. So I blamed my mum when I felt or saw those parts in me that reminded me of her. Working with spirit and my intuition has taught me otherwise. Working with wild women and goddesses like Kali the goddess of death, Inanna the Sumerian goddess, and Hela the Nordic giant of the realm of death have led the way for me in holding my ground. They have taught me not to fear my power but to recognise it. The life force that lives within me is valuable and magical, and it is my job to be deliberate with it.

What is your relationship with boundaries like?

What empowers you to use your voice?

What situations silence you?

Is there an area of your life where you would like to practice using and enforcing boundaries?

Are you afraid of your own power?

CHAPTER 18

INTO THE WILD

"Intuition is the treasure of a woman's psyche.
It is the divining instrument and like a crystal through
which one can see with uncanny interior vision.
It is like a wise old woman who is with you always,
who tells you exactly what the matter is,
tells you exactly whether you need to go left or right.
It is a form of The One Who Knows,
old La Que Sabe, the Wild Woman."
- CLARISSA PINKOLA ESTÉS

Moving to Austin in early 2019, just a few weeks after my green card interview in Montreal, was a giant leap forward for me. The last time I moved to be with Faris, I was more or less running away from my life, my ex, and my mum in Vancouver to live in Dubai. This time I was choosing a life consciously. I was choosing to fully commit to my marriage, and live in a city that deeply called me. The gruelling process of getting a green card really tested me and took me through a sticky exercise of really evaluating my desires. I was at a point where I knew that I either had to be all in and face my fears, or give up completely. We had work to do together, and that work required us to live together in the same country.

A few months after the big move I was walking down East 7th street on the way home from coffee with my friend Jamie, listening to a podcast with Brené Brown. She was talking about safety and trust, and in that moment, there was a part of me that felt unsafe. A voice popped into my head, "You can't run away from your problems." I listened to Brené Brown's words, watching them fall into my heart space and nestle into my body very easily. They resonated. SCRATCH! I spun around and looked up. A shiny, blue and black grackle was flying in the other direction, shaking its tail feathers at me as if it were laughing. For some reason, it felt called to fly down to me and hit me in the head rather blatantly. Some might call this an attack. I call it a message, a wake up call. The grackle was rather rudely nudging me into the present moment and out of my head in a more gentle way than the car did in Vancouver a few years prior. I've always felt close to birds, and from the moment that I moved to Austin, I was intrigued by these crow-like birds called grackles. They talk a lot, making a "grackle"-like noise that sounds more like a witchy cackle. Much like crows and ravens, they are feared and misunderstood, probably because of their dark colour. To me, they are mystical, magical, and otherworldly. We don't have crows and ravens

"There is peaceful.
There is wild.
I am both and at the same time."

- SUM

in Austin, so I feel like grackles are their close cousins, reminding me of that connection. I pulled my earphones out, took a deep breath, and continued walking forward. I got the message. It was time to be more present than I had ever been before

Intuition is a whisper that requires silencing the loud noises of the mind in order to hear it. The whispers of intuition require silence. It is a calling back to ourselves and our true desires. For me, it is a calling into the wild. My intuition is what brought my awareness back to my thoughts. It was a slow climb out of the crevasse of purging and self-harm, but with each day, I was able to uncover myself and hear my inner voice. When my mind was busiest, the only break I would get from it was through drinking or bingeing. Addictions have a way of numbing out the fear and giving us a temporary feeling of relief from the pain. The only way through was to sever the part of me that couldn't handle the intensity of what I felt. I needed to open up the space to feel it all by increasing the bandwidth of what I could hold. I needed to find comfort in silence. When we experience challenges, we increase our ability to hold energy. In order to hold it, though, we need to be fully present with it. If we are at all numbing ourselves, or hiding what we feel to fake our strength, that emotion is going to come back around in some way. This is part of why people say that the most powerful healers are the ones who know deep pain. When someone has walked through the cave of darkness, you will know, because when they walk with you or stand there with you, you feel fully seen, held, and safe. They aren't trying to get away from it, judge it, make it smaller, or pretend it isn't there. They are simply there, in the darkness, with you. Just like the ravens who sat with me.

I have always felt most myself when I have stripped down to the basics—messy hair, dirty, and uninhibited as if I've just returned from a day outside with the horses. And for me, my intuition brought me back to this place, a place I lost for 15 years. I've always strayed off the mainstream path literally and energetically, sometimes to my husband's dismay. When I'm leading the way, you can almost guarantee that you will be in the bushes with some possible scrapes and ripped clothes in no time. You will be up close and intimate with nature—feeling her touch, hearing her song, and smelling her scent. I might even ask you to stop talking, so you can listen to the silence. Once I started listening, my feet would always guide me into these spaces. Our internal guidance will take us places that do not make sense. It will take us off course and onto paths that are barely there. But if we are listening, we will always find what is there for us.

The journey is truly the prescription to finding the truth. We can't skip through the pages of the book, missing the details, expecting to find the deep message. We can't skip through the uncomfortable emotions to arrive healed. We must feel it all. We must be willing to read each line, each word, and feel the space in between. I used to love skipping ahead in books. I used to read books by reading a page, paying attention to how fast I would read it, and then look ahead to see how many pages were left in the chapter and how many more chapters were left in the book. This journey isn't about going fast. It is about feeling it all—dark and light, death and life, grief and joy. We can't truly be with our intuition if we are hiding parts of ourselves.

In my journey, as I have ventured deeper into the layers of intuition and my ancestry, the call to the wild has merely increased. Learning about these parts of myself that I kept hidden creates a desire to meet the women who have done this too. My craving for the wild, emboldened women is strong and I search for their stories, symbols, and imprints everywhere. In this search, I have recognised that a lot of these stories are also hidden behind other stories, perhaps less honest and more biased stories that are told through a masculine lens.

"A soft woman is simply a wolf caught in meditation."

- PAVANA

In Nordic mythology, I rarely hear of the giants. Everyone always talks about Odin and Thor, the great gods. The only time I hear of giants, like Angrboda is in the old tale of Loki and how he angered the gods by mating with her in the forbidden forest and having their three despicable children, Fenrir the wolf, Jormungand the death-eating serpent, and Hela, the keeper of Hell. Angrboda is purely known as the ugly, unwanted giant who brought these horrible children into the world. The moment I heard the story of Angrboda and learned more about who she was, I loved her. She felt powerful, rebellious, and best of all, she was always pictured with wolves by her side. She was the mother of the most feared wolf and shapeshifter, Fenrir. She was wild. And she was a witch. When we are told stories, we look for ourselves in them, in their journeys, experiences, and characteristics. When little girls grow up looking for their "less desirable" traits in stories of other women, only to find that they are either hidden or frowned upon, they learn to hide their own. In our world, we need more stories about women like Angrboda, and we need them to be told from her perspective.

As I dive deeper into Norse mythology and the world of the Nornir, I continue to meet so many incredible beings who are living in the darkness. Skadi, my favourite, is the giantess of winter, who always has a bow and arrow in tow and wolves by her side. She is the huntress, brave beyond knowing, and deeply rooted in mother nature's wisdom and resilience. She is ferocious, deliberate, and independent. There's Hyndla, an old hag who is the embodiment of ancestry.com. She holds the wisdom of all blood lines and knows who you are and where you have come from. She is connected to the rune Othila, which asks us the questions of who we are, which lands we come from, and what our truth is. There is Hyrokkin, the giantess who is known for her incredible strength. She is pictured with a big horse who can transform into a wolf who she controls with reins made of poisonous snakes, and she lives in the dark forest in Jotunheim. In her story, she is summoned to Asgard by the gods to help drag a ship out to sea when no one else is strong enough for the task. She does the impossible task unphased with one hand. In her stories, she is depicted as hideous and ugly as is Angrboda. Instead of Disney princesses, these are my role models and guides in life. They are wise, wild, and free. They have been forgotten because they haven't fit in the boxes of our world. They haven't changed or sacrificed themselves to be loved and accepted.

Little girls are brought up learning that in order to be loved they must be beautiful, agreeable, easy going, and fun. They cannot show any side of themselves that will challenge or threaten that illusion, and if they do, they will lose. They will lose love, security, stability, and safety. I feel that Angrboda isn't mentioned much in the stories because she isn't beautiful and easy on the eyes. She angered the gods, and she brought darkness into the world. Her presence disrupted the peace; she charmed the trickster god into being her beloved and brought the uncontrollable wild into the world. She was a shapeshifter, a rebel, and a rule breaker. She wasn't there to please or bring ease and light into the world. This isn't to say that she isn't light or love; she and Loki fell in love and they had children whom they loved deeply. Angrboda invites the dark side of love. She mothered three monsters and loved them entirely. She brings transformation in the most powerful manner; she is a challenger. So often we think of mother nature as serene, peaceful, beautiful, and balanced. However, mother nature has many sides, and she is not always gentle. In fact, she is rarely gentle. Even in the ocean, despite the serenity that it gives off, beneath the surface it is dark, deep, and unknown. It is lovely to watch the waves, but it is deeply uncomfortable and life-threatening to be pulled into the current. Nature can be gentle or fierce, save lives or kill. Angrboda birthed three beasts into the world who were deeply misunderstood because of their darkness and, consequently, condemned.

Each of her children represent the shadow side of the world, showing us the parts of ourselves that we need to reclaim.

In the past year of my life, I feel as though I have met the love of Angrboda. I always had this dream of the life I craved, and it included dogs. Dogs that I had such a deep and intimate connection with, the type of relationship that you witness and envy. I dreamt of walking to cafes with my dogs, parking them outside to wait, and enjoying the day together in peace. Envisioning us exploring the wild, them running around, untethered. I dreamt of a relationship that was rooted in respect and good communication, one where I understood them and they understood me. Somewhere in this dreaming, my mind got involved and brought with it perfectionism and control. Instead of seeing the dream in my reality, I began to see the flaws. Instead of dogs that were perfect, I have dogs that challenge me. Instead of easy dogs that display behaviours that make people smile, I have dogs that bark, react, and challenge me. Our animals reflect us, and oftentimes, they can show us the shadow sides of life.

I'm drawn to women and teachers who feel ancient. When I interact with them, I see beyond the illusion of their physical appearance. I feel the power of their journeys, and I know from being with them that they have walked the talk. They are the mystics, the ones who are living intuitively, and they don't teach something that they aren't being. They aren't scared of the dark; they welcome it as a friend and partner.

Are you drawn to the wild?

Have you connected to your inner wild self?

What stories, folklore, and myths are you most drawn to?

What teachers do you feel connected to?

When you are in the wild, how do you feel?

What characters were you drawn to as a child?

What stories shaped you?

CHAPTER 19

TURNING AWAY FROM TRUTH

"It is said that the gods do not talk to us anymore
because we no longer believe in them."
– INGRID KINCAID

I marched myself into the back closet of our Austin apartment and slammed the door in a tantrum. I threw myself onto the cream-coloured rough carpet, folding my torso over my legs and bending my knees. I dipped my head between my legs, forcing my breath to create space between myself and my thoughts. It had been weeks of feeling this way, and I was on the edge. I couldn't handle the pressure that I felt anymore. I wanted to run away and hide from the world, and I wanted everything and everyone to leave me alone. The responsibilities of clients, readings, classes, and workshops were too much. No matter what I did, or focused on, the unwanted electricity that I felt in my body wouldn't leave me. I craved a dark small space that felt safe. Like my dog Ollie during thunderstorms, my body took me to the closet—the darkest, smallest space in the house. Although I was 30 years old, other parts of me were present, other ages. This feeling was familiar. I had been here before, unknowingly. None of the luminous colours of my hanging clothes were a match for the darkness, and they simply drowned in it. They couldn't change the shadow of the darkness that I felt inside. This week, it felt inescapable. Nothing moved it—not painting, writing, sleeping, meditating, bathing, or eating. Everywhere I went, it followed. I felt like an uncontrollable mess.

Once I decided to be a psychic and do the work, my life didn't instantaneously transform. I didn't suddenly live every waking hour in alignment. Instead, my awareness was much greater. When the waves of challenge came, I couldn't ignore them like I once did. I couldn't out-party them, or out sleep them. I had to face them. Before, I created a life that didn't rely on me showing up. I barely went to classes in University, and my attendance rate at jobs was poor. The moment a shadow came knocking on my door, I would surrender, succumb, and let it swallow me whole. Sometimes I would spend a whole week closed up in my bedroom hiding. I couldn't do that anymore. With the life that I created, I had people to show up for: my husband, my family, my friends, my pets, my clients. To this day, I still have moments when it's challenging to show up consistently and completely. When things go "wrong" it's so easy to throw in the towel and surrender to the story. It's so tempting. Now, when I reschedule clients or turn down plans, there's a level of responsibility and integrity that I'm aware of. As my mum always said to me, every choice has an outcome and every move creates consequence. Sometimes it is a balancing act between honouring my commitments and honouring my truth, and the "answer" isn't always obvious and it is never about right or wrong. I know that the more I resist the wave of transformation that is clearly upon me, the deeper the hole becomes, that I will soon have to climb out of. It's a blessing to have a career that is rooted around being in service because it takes me out of my story and back into my heart so much faster.

This time though, during one hot and gloomy June in Austin during my first summer there, that part of me that fights my joy and success came knocking on my door, and I let her in. I called it my "June-uary," despite the fact that the sweltering Texas heat was everything but gloomy. I couldn't shake what I felt. I rescheduled clients again and again and again for a whole week. I felt lost and stuck like a large weight was pressing down on my chest, holding me under. The problem was that whenever I got myself into slight balance that was the moment something went "wrong." I spiralled back into an out-of-control frenzy. It was as if somehow I had been transplanted back into high school, and the rebellious Chloe who was in extreme pain and couldn't understand any of what she was feeling was here and ready to fight to the death. When I was in high school, even though my mum was around, I mostly felt like I was in charge of myself. I didn't really feel like I had a solid adult to count on. I had no boundaries. So in these moments when I was faced with fear, I would succumb to the feelings, which usually meant not showing up to my commitments. If I ever felt vulnerable or inadequate, I would return to my shell and hide.

I pushed Faris's tender arms off of me, pushing away his love. He joined me in the closet on the floor, unsure of what to do. This wasn't the first time that Faris had witnessed me in a pool of emotions and overwhelming psychic energy, and it wasn't the first time that he was at a loss of what to do to help me. He handed my phone to me and desperately offered his words of saving grace, "Text Lynnette." I disregarded what he said, shoving the phone towards the floor. I wanted to stay here. Faris and Ollie left the closet, leaving me with my phone and a choice. Here I was, another moment in the darkness, on the floor, with the option of an elder to help me. I grabbed my phone, wiping my tears and snot from my face and sent the text. She responded within seconds as if she was already with me in the room. There I sat, in the dark, with Lynnette talking through what was here. She didn't push; she didn't try to solve, and she didn't leave. She stayed with me, listening and asking questions. Within minutes, after over two weeks of being here, she asked me the question, "Have you been here before? What do you see?" There it was. Sixteen year old Chloe was here, in the closet with me, and she was suffering. She was fighting for protection. She was scared and felt vulnerable.

This was a quality that stood out to me in the elders I was drawn to. The first time I really noticed it was in Maui with my mum at the silent retreat with Gangaji. I noticed that Gangaji would always sit there with the people who came on stage to share their stories and pain. Some of these people were in deep states of trauma and pain, and regardless of who came up, she remained in that space of being in her center. She didn't change because of their stories. I once heard that a true healer will sit with you in the darkness without trying to take you out of it. I always loved that story because I felt it too. Why would you try to pull someone out of their darkness when it is a deep state of richness. If you are trying to pull someone out, perhaps it is because you are projecting your own fear and discomfort of the darkness onto them and their situation. I want to be in the darkness and sit with others who can be there too, without trying to leave or turn on the lights. To be there and ask the questions and recognise that every place comes with its wisdom and medicine.

We don't always listen, and to this day, I still have moments when I hear guidance, keep going, and receive a rather obvious poke from my guides. This moment in the closet was one of those pokes. I was watching a music video on Youtube, and I saw an ad for a video on dog training. The moment I saw it, I knew that watching it before bed could activate fear and anxiety, and I heard a voice in my head telling me just that. I ignored the voice and clicked on the video. Just as it was loading, I leaned back onto my pillow, and my laptop screen fell forward and hit me in the face. It busted my lip, but I got the message.

The more we feel, the further we can go into the depths of our darkness. Even after saying "yes" to intuition and to following my truth, I have had moments of intense darkness and I've trapped myself there. When you're in a new place that you've never been to before, it's easy to get lost. The further you go and the more turns you take, the more lost you feel and the greater your fear is. That is exactly how it can feel when you start to dive into your intuition. Everything that has kept you from it in the past reveals itself. All of the fears envelop you and stick to you like a spider's web. When you take a turn that you haven't taken before, chances of getting caught in older webs are high. Interwoven thoughts, stories, beliefs, fears, and memories that have been sitting in the dark, untouched and unfelt. That's how I felt when I began intentionally working with my intuition and coming out of the psychic closet. The first few years was a combination of highs and lows, filled with a lot of doubt, fear, and insecurity. There was a part of me that knew that I was on the right track and that I was psychic, but there was another very loud part of me that was completely against it. I felt like I wasn't strong, good, or committed enough to make it happen. I compared myself a lot to others and looked for all of the ways that they were better than me. I mostly discounted the moments that were easy. When I received confirmation and validation of my gifts, I focused solely on the moments I felt like a failure or when things felt hard.

I began to feel remorseful for how I spent the last few years of high school. I wished that I hadn't spent so much time alone in bed or laying around watching movies and digging dark holes of sadness and depression. I saw that doing that for so long had created a pattern of comfort and resistance, a way for me to stay in fear and work against myself. Even though it seemed like I was resting and being lazy, I was actually soaking in sabotage and self-hatred. As I stayed in that place, I grew more tired and the distance between me and my truth widened.

I've witnessed this happen several times in the work that I do. Once someone makes the decision to go for it and begin working as a psychic and honour the gifts and desires that they have felt deeply for some time, life begins to bring unexpected things forward that stop them in their tracks. Similar to when someone begins to do the inner work for the first time, what they begin to see and feel can catapult them into a space that is extremely uncomfortable and confrontational.

These moments are referred to as the "dark nights of the soul." They are times when you go through a form of existential crisis and begin to question everything. This term was first introduced by 16th century Spanish mystic and poet St. John of the Cross. Life begins to feel meaningless, and as you question everything, you find yourself wandering deeper into a state of inescapable darkness. The purpose that you previously felt comes crashing down and the structures that you have built around you as support, collapse. There are many ways to activate this state of being, and essentially, it is a time of deep transformation. It can be triggered by a big change like the death of a loved one, the end of a relationship, or losing a job. I see it as we are being thrown in the washing machine to clear out and clean up what is no longer needed. There are many ways to look at how and when a dark night of the soul occurs, but it is something that happens with purpose. It is a sobering time, when everything is brought to the table to look at who you are being, who you have been, what you are doing, and what you have done. In many ways, the term "dark night of the soul" is another way that we villainize darkness. It is rarely a time that we welcome and celebrate, just as we immediately turn on the lights when the sun sets without truly experiencing the arrival of the night. Similar to shadow work in psychology and spirituality, it's always portrayed as a very heavy, unwelcome, and inescapable state. Darkness is oftentimes referred to as the absence of light, rather than its own being. A shadow is always referred to as a representation of darkness. The truth is, shadows are created in the daylight, not at night. Shadows are created when light is blocked by an object or projected over an object, creating a shadow. When we make these states negative, we deny ourselves their true offerings. Like all emotions, they hold their own unique purpose. Our world sees depression as something that is wrong and needs to be fixed. But what if depression has just as much purpose as joy? When we make something bad, it's easy to get stuck there. The more sensitive we are, the more we feel and the more we have hidden from feeling. Like those months that I spent hiding on my red couch in Malaysia, we tend to build a mountain of emotions that we believe we can't handle. Climbing that mountain, once we recognise that we've built it, seems nearly impossible. It takes our courage, bravery, and commitment to their greatest capacities. They challenge us more than anything else and require meeting ourselves in a way that we never have before. It requires being the ultimate source of love and support for ourselves and ending the external search for it. It takes us to a place of dying so that we can be reborn.

What is your spiralling moment?

Where in your life are you not telling yourself the truth?

Are there any truths that you are avoiding or scared of acknowledging?

What happens when you sit with truth?

What feelings do you deny yourself?

When do you feel like your power is outside of you?

"The universe is not outside of you.
Look inside yourself; everything that you want, you already are."

- RUMI

CHAPTER 20

MELDED BY THE FLAME

"How is it that in our ignorance we have forgotten
that she who gives us light can also blind us."
- INGRID KINCAID

Moths are the allies of darkness and seekers of light. They emerge with the sun's departure and aggressively search for sources of light to guide them. Every single lamppost and light bulb would be surrounded by them, flying around in circles like a bunch of chickens with their heads cut off—directionless and wild. Their movement was erratic and without purpose. I would do anything I could to stay away from them and their swarm. Seeing them would make my skin crawl and my stomach flip. Their wings were breakable and delicate like thin layers of silk or dried caramel. Their bodies were black and ant-like. Some would be crawling on the floor, wingless and disabled, by the heat of the light bulb. Moths use the moonlight to help them fly in a straight line. Similar to how we use the north star as our compass when we need a sense of direction. Prior to man-made lighting, moths and other insects would fly towards the moonlight as a way to find direction and purpose. Now, people wonder if moths are suicidal, flying directly into light to their death. With the moths in Malaysia, many of them would die every night. In the mornings, we would be greeted by a massacre of dead flying ant bodies underneath all of the lampposts. By late morning, the bodies would be cleared and cleaned up by mother nature's rain and wind, or by the gardeners.

Can we find our way without light? Can we move with purpose in pure darkness? And what happens if we fly full-force directly into the sunlight? Do we burn and die? If we only focus on the light, the ease, and the perfection, we can lose our balance in this world and lose our way. We cannot expect to only live in the light. There is nothing beautiful about perfection. I continue to witness an old and impractical standard of perfection that I hold over myself. What a destructive and unrealistic standard to hold onto. When I consciously notice this thought pattern re-emerge, I realize how silly it truly is. No one lives their life in complete perfection in every moment. It's impossible. This image of perfection in itself is an illusion. We must accept that as humans, we live in the flicker—the flicker of dark and light.

The cycle of expecting to be perfect, only living in the light, was constant, continuous, and exhausting. It kept me from healing. It was obsessive. I would binge and purge and then go through hell to pick myself back up, get re-centered, feel good, and go right back into the cycle again and again. Like the moth, I would go towards the light only to die and have my ant-like body lying on the ground the next day for the gardeners to sweep away. Having the goal of perfection, the light only burned me.

I avoided change. Change was my enemy and a powerful challenger to my desire for control. Change shakes everything up, like shaking a snow globe. Change creates new realities. In ways, I feel that we have been blinded by our obsession with the light. We have been conditioned to fear darkness and to relate anything that is dark as bad or unwanted. By referring to darkness as a creation of the light, we disempower darkness and belittle it. It used to take a lot of darkness to stop me. I towed the line, as they say. Sometimes, this meant a lot of struggle; I ignored my guidance and avoided the discomfort of truth and change. This denial meant that in order to get a message across to me, energy would have to come at me full force. Sometimes, I would get nudged several times before I paid attention to what was going on around me. My desensitization and emotional shutdown wasn't doing me any favours. It was a source of a lot of my suffering, and I had no awareness of it. Sometimes, we hold onto a fairy tale idea so strongly that we miss the beauty of our reality.

My cycles of relapse usually occurred after drinking, partying, or experiencing change. As I started to break my track of perfection and control with binge-and-purge cycles, I would go into a deep spiral of shame, guilt, and judgment. I was brought right back to where I started, feeling like a failure and completely unworthy of love. It was never-ending and consumed my life for at least ten years. I was obsessed about getting it completely right and living in the light, and perhaps, that was me flying into the light as a moth and continually failing, dying in the fake light that wasn't the moon.

One night, I heard a voice. Everything was as it always was: I had just binged and purged after a night out and a day of staying at home. I went through analysis (and shame) of everything that occurred the night before. I reached for food, TV shows, and isolation as a source of comfort and punishment. Punishment was an uncomfortable and familiar place for me, and I was about to step deeper into the cycle. I was hot, uncomfortable, and angry with myself. My body felt like a heated balloon. And then a voice appeared in my head, "What if this is meaningless? What if you chose to do something different this time and let yourself off the hook? What if you actually haven't done anything wrong? What if this shitty feeling doesn't mean anything about you?" The questions showered through my mind, one after the other, in a very peaceful progression. The voice stopped me on my way to the bathroom like a tiny light illuminating a room of darkness. It took a few minutes to adjust my eyes to this new reality being presented. The same way our eyes adjust when someone suddenly turns the light on in our bedroom after a night of sleep.

The voice was asking me to call a truce—the competitors were me versus me. I had to choose something different, and this new way of thinking felt exciting, slightly risky, and extremely out of the blue. It was an option, something that I had the freedom to choose. Instead of diving back into the dark hole that I knew so well, I decided to change. That night, I chose to let it be what it was, without meaning. I didn't make my purging mean relapse, failure, or unworthiness. I let it be what it was, just something that happened. For the first time, I accepted both my dark and light co-existing in my body. I shed my old beliefs and welcomed in new ones. I felt safe, abundant, and powerful. My body knew exactly what it wanted and needed. I was able to accept myself for my flaws, and slowly, my relapses were fewer.

The bridge that connects us between our past self and our desired self is one that takes time to build and, sometimes, even more time to cross. Sometimes, it seems like we continue to circle around the same issue without ever feeling something different or creating a new outcome. This is part of the healing process. In my relationship with Faris, there were many moments when I felt that nothing was changing, and we were continuously butting heads on the same issues. What I came to know is that everytime I would revisit a pattern, something small would shift. Sometimes, the change was so subtle that it really required my presence to be with it and acknowledge it. I notice this same frustration in clients when they are working on something that has deep roots. Change is not always clear or obvious to the naked eye, and we have to practice listening for the subtle hints of movement. When you plant a seed in your garden, it will take time before you notice growth. Underneath the soil, a lot is taking place, but above soil it all seems the same. If you overwater, or get impatient, you could end up slowing down the growth or even killing it.

When it comes to change, we are always walking up or down a spiral staircase. Although it seems like we are visiting the same place again and again, the truth is that every time we are looking at it from a slightly different perspective. When we are with ourselves all of the time, it's not as easy to gauge the small changes. Just like seeing someone after some time of not seeing them, you notice more than if you were to see them every day. For a long time, my healing journey with my eating disorder, depression, and feeling lost felt like finding a needle in a haystack. No matter how hard I tried and how much effort I put into it, nothing seemed to change. It was always a two steps forward, four steps back type of situation. As soon as I felt like I was getting somewhere, I would be hit with an overwhelming desire to destroy everything. I was constantly putting my life back together and then fucking it up all over again. I was always searching for something to change how I felt, and nothing that I found quite fit the bill because it was always outside of me. I was searching for whatever would solve my problems, satiate my hunger, or confirm my fear that there was something wrong with me. I had shut my intuition down and severed my connection to myself, and until I returned there, the desperate search would continue.

Nothing was truly going to change until I learned how to be with myself and be all that I needed. Instead of feeling something and going to an external source to answer the desire, I needed to discover that source inside of me. Instead of immediately picking up my phone and texting a friend, or finding someone who was going to help me feel better, I needed to discover that love inside of me. This is where the real work began. Before I started working with Dr. Divi and Lynette, everything was a Band-Aid. I was always relying on things outside of myself to keep me together. I had to learn to stand in my center and hold my ground. This was foreign to me. My life had become a desperate search for stability, but the problem was that I didn't believe in it, so the moment it became real, I would demolish it before it could hurt me.

At first, working with emotions and beginning to embrace them felt like circling the drain, waiting to fall in. It soon became clear why I often felt like a balloon was about to burst. I felt so much, and I didn't allow myself to feel. I soon learned that emotions are energy in motion, and so when we don't feel them, they stay where they are. They don't move, unless we allow them to. And you can feel when an emotion moves. You feel it in your body. When we shut down our energy centers and reject our feelings, we become swollen energetic blobs of emotion.

I often find myself in conversations with others about emotions and what is considered a healthy or acceptable expression. It is impossible to express anger in a way that it feels controlled and orderly. You can't package anger in delightful wrapping paper, complete with a pretty bow. Anger is fire. Fire is untamed and uncontrollable. For so long, I hid my emotions and compartmentalised them into the categories of good and bad. Anything that resembled how my mum was, was bad. Evidently, I had many outbursts that reflected what I witnessed in my mum. I started to notice this same conflict in my brother Sam in our late twenties. Up until then, he had done a pretty good job of disguising his trauma from our childhood through music, dreadlocks, sports, and smoking weed. Once Sam really started his healing work and joined a men's group, it didn't mean that it all healed spontaneously. In spiritual self work, when you bring your awareness to an area that has been hidden, it usually results in it all coming out like a glass overflowing with water. These are the moments when the work really begins—to be with everything that you've been hiding from.

My brother was on a holiday with his fiancée and her family, and they had an argument during their last night together. Something about this interaction activated his old anger, and he yelled at his in-laws. The next morning he felt an incredible amount of judgment and shame. I reminded him of what he already knew, that anger isn't something to feel shame about and that every emotion has a purpose. When we express our emotions, it leaves us raw, open, and vulnerable, and that isn't always a very comfortable experience. We try our best to be "civilised" but in each of us lives a wild beast. Anger is fiery, and when it moves, it creates a clearing for something new. Up until I began working with my intuition, around the same time that I met Dr. Divi, the only time when my emotions were expressed was when I was drinking. Alcohol was the only thing that would drop my inhibitions, and because of who I am and how I approached my emotions, I was basically a walking loaded gun. The moment something poked me the wrong way, I would lose control and spin into chaos.

I began to realise that an eating disorder is a perfect tool to shut down intuition. When we attempt to control and manipulate our bodies, we are controlling the divine vessel within, which we receive information. This is something that I've noticed over time and continue to notice in the people who I work with. We learn that our emotions are not accepted, embraced, or celebrated in our world. For those of us who feel deeply, it is seen as a handicap and something that affects our worthiness, level of success, and survival in the world.

I have found that many people who are deeply emotional and energetically sensitive hold the cellular memory in their bodies of lifetimes when they have been persecuted, oppressed, and even killed for being emotional, sensitive, intuitive, and intimately connected to nature. The fear of this memory lives within them, directing who they are and how they operate in this lifetime.

This is something that began to show up in my reality, especially after I started to work professionally as a psychic. The way that I learned to understand it, is that my lifetimes and timelines would cross over, and I would essentially feel like I was revisiting somewhere I had been before, or meeting someone I knew, even though I had no evidence of that from my current lifetime. The moments where this was strongest was during travel. When Faris and I did a road trip from DC to Atlanta, the year before I moved to Austin, the moment we arrived in Charleston, South Carolina, I felt a sensation of familiarity. The morning after our arrival, Faris woke up early to work and I agreed to join him a few hours later, once I finished my client sessions. When I left the Airbnb, instead of looking at my map, I felt as though I already knew where I was going. Somehow, I found my way to the cafe, which was at least 15 minutes away, without checking the map. I turned when I heard "left" or "right" and walked straight when I felt a sense of calm. Sometimes, my soul experiences in other countries have not been as pleasant and playful. During one of our trips, we stopped in Latvia for the night, as per Faris' efficient flight itinerary. The moment we arrived in Latvia, I felt really uncomfortable and nauseous. That night, I didn't sleep. I was in the bathroom, vomiting, crying, and shaking. Instead of waking up Faris, I stayed in the bathroom, in the darkness, suffering alone. The information that I received the following morning was that being in Latvia triggered a previous lifetime to emerge into my experience where I had been poisoned and then burned at the stake during the Baltic witch trials in Latvia, and I was left alone to die. Luckily we flew out that morning, and I couldn't get out of there fast enough.

Another traumatising experience was when I joined Faris in Las Palmas where he had been working and living for a few weeks. The moment I arrived on the island, I felt like I shouldn't be there and I wanted to leave. The day after I arrived, the apartment where Faris was staying had major plumbing issues and the floor drain in the courtyard started to overflow with dirty, stinky sewage. I had to leave, while the plumber came and I walked around the main town for a few hours. During that walk, I felt as though I was walking in between timelines and kept seeing interesting symbols on the walls and in my vision. It was as if I was no longer standing in the 21st century. I followed my intuition into the local bookstore and found myself sitting on the floor in a corner, grabbing a few books from the shelves. To my shock, all of the books were on witches and the witch trials that happened in Spain in the 1500s. Most of the books were in Spanish, but from what I gathered, some women fled to Las Palmas to escape the witch trials, and many were found, murdered, and burned at the stake. Others were never to be heard of again. I left Las Palmas the next day. I continued to experience things like this over that two-year period of first labeling myself as a psychic and doing the work. Interestingly, at the time, I was also hosting the event series back in Vancouver called The Witchery, which was rooted in magic and the gathering of witches. Clearly, I was working through whatever pain and trauma was keeping me from standing in my center as a witch. To this day, whenever I am speaking in front of a new group, my throat gets tight and my body gets very warm. As a child, instead of learning to heal and work through these experiences, I shut down and closed off out of fear. I now know that these experiences come up to support us and guide us into our power rather than solely serving to destabilize us and stop us from stepping forward into our gifts and work.

What is your relationship with change?

When you look back at your life, what moments stand out to you?

Standing where you are now, do you have a clearer sense of the purpose of some of the contrast you experienced?

Have you connected to your past lives before?

Do you ever experience moments where a sudden, random image or vision of you flashes into your mind but it isn't from this lifetime?

What do you know or believe about your past lives?

Are there places that you've traveled to and experienced spiritual moments?

CHAPTER 21

SEEING IN THE DARK

"Do not let your handful of light sting the eyes
of those who have bathed in darkness."
- CHRISTINE VALTERS PAINTNER

A week after returning from Marfa I sat in my living room alone in the darkness, and they came. The dogs sensed them first. Blue emerged from a deep, snoring slumber and gently coughed under his breath—something that he does when he is aware of an intruder in his space, offering a warning. Ollie followed in a less subtle way, more startled by the obvious disturbance. His bark brought my awareness away from the page. The fan and the fan light which sat dormant above me suddenly turned on with no reason behind it. The fluorescent light alerted me immediately, knowing that there was no logical reasoning behind this electrical mishap. The light turned off as fast as it turned on, and then again and again five times. The fan then switched on and off and on in the same manner, shifting speeds randomly. This time, I wasn't scared. As the lights flashed on and off like a broken traffic light, I breathed in the essence of their familiar presence. I leaned over to switch off the lamp beside me and grabbed my shiny black lighter.

I lit the candle and it flickered as the elders crowded into our living room. They were all here, encircling me with their comforting and bossy persistence. I knew them immediately; we had met before at a time when I wasn't ready to face the truth that they brought with them. This time, I blew out the candle and sat there with them in the darkness, listening to what they had to say. Fanny, Jane, Alice, Eliza, Mercy…my ancestors, the women who have walked before me from my mum's lineage. The women who hold the stories of my blood. This moment brought me back to my time at the ranch when I was alone with them three years ago when they first showed themselves to me. That time, I wasn't calm. I was terrified and couldn't be with them. I asked them to leave, despite my best efforts to speak to them. At the time, I was no match for the darkness which invited them. This time, the darkness felt different. Instead of intruders, they felt like guests, and instead of fear, I felt love and intrigue. I didn't need to run away, or chase them away with obnoxious lights and noise. I breathed in their presence, blew out the candle, and sat there with them, listening. The next morning I created my ancestor altar to honour them.

A quick google search on darkness or quotes on darkness quickly reveals our backwards and negative relationship with darkness. It is either depicted as this shameful and terrorizing space, or it is put beside light as the part that exemplifies the light. Darkness is its own being. Without the meaning and judgement that we attach to it, it stands alone as a divine expression of source. It's possible that our relationship with darkness became tainted with the creation of religion and patriarchy. Anything associated with darkness suddenly became shameful, sinful, and evil. We were taught to judge and reject any part of ourselves that resembled darkness. Our own darkness was put into a box and shoved into a forbidden closet.

In the story of Adam and Eve, they are punished by God for ignoring his plea for them not to eat the fruit from the trees. Eve is tempted into doing so by a mischievous serpent, and she shares the forbidden fruit with Adam. They are both punished, and Eve is seen as the source of the original sin, sentenced to a life of painful childbirth and subservience to her husband. In the story, they are described as naked and vulnerable, and they work to hide their vulnerabilities with plant leaves. Some have argued that this part of the story is the origin of the "shadow self;" our naked and most vulnerable part of ourselves is also our shameful source of darkness. By creating this foundation of control where shame is the tool, it is easy to keep others out of their power. It is time for us all to explore our inner darkness and create the space where we can embrace our darkness and share it with the world. It is not just a partner to the light. It is time for us to look at the belief systems and stories that we hold about darkness.

Deep down, I am reminded: I am who I am and my journey has been about re-becoming my innate self. I know I've been scared to truly be seen as myself in the past. I've felt too big, too emotional, too intense, too sensitive, and too loud. I know that it hasn't felt safe. I know that it hasn't felt acceptable. I've changed that. I've changed that for many people. For so long, I've had glimpses of a life that I craved. And by trying to fit into the box that I was given, I shut down those dreams. I forgot them. I pretended that they were no longer there and I was not worthy of them. I ran away from the dark and all of the magic that it brought with it.

I often wake up in the mornings hearing songs. For many years, I thought nothing of it and moved through my day slowly drowning out the wisdom of the music. Now, when I hear a song, I listen. As I pull the thread of what I sense, a message reveals itself to me. A message from my ancestors and guides, whether it's the lyrics of the song, the feeling of the song itself, or my memory of the song. I grew up in a musical family and music is a big way that my ancestors communicate with me.

One morning, I woke up hearing the music to a song that felt both haunting and intimate. I decided to have a shower and allow the water flow to bring the song into the present moment. It took me a few minutes of singing it and feeling the words that were hiding in the silence. I immediately felt my mum and grandpa's energy with me. They both played this song on the piano. I realised that I had been feeling my grandpa's energy with me the day before too and fell asleep feeling a presence in the bedroom. When I spoke to my mum about it later in the day, she too had felt her dad around her and dreamt of me singing the song to her. We also realised that it was his birthday. The music that I heard was the theme song of the old christmas movie "The Snowman." This was a movie that my brother and I watched every year growing up. I remembered that the movie confused me because I loved it, and it scared

"Learn the alchemy true human beings know.
The moment you accept what troubles you've been given,
the door will open."

- RUMI

me. That day, I rewatched the 28 minute movie to remember. The boy builds a snowman in the daytime, and at night, he watches the snowman magically come to life. They spend the night together, playing inside and outside and the snowman takes him flying in the sky on a journey to the north pole. At the end of the movie, the boy wakes up in the morning and runs outside to realise that the snowman is gone. The snowman died, and he left behind the buttons, hat, and scarf atop a mound of snow. I sat with the movie, trying to remember what about it exactly scared me. Was it that the snowman came to life in the night, or was it that it died in the end? Was it because the snowman could only live in the dark? Everything that the boy felt and witnessed that night with his snowman was to be kept a secret. His parents would never believe him as if it never even happened. I thought about how many times I kept secrets from my parents, both because I was scared of how they'd react and because I felt that they were meant to be secrets. How often do we hide our spiritual experiences inside? When we witness magic, we feel as though we have to hide it. We bury those experiences inside our subconscious, hiding the magic that was shared with us. I stopped believing in Santa Claus before my brother did. The moment that I caught my dad snacking on carrots and sipping red wine on Christmas Eve when I was six, I shut down the part of me that wanted to believe in the story that I loved so much. I remember feeling more mature than my brother for finding out the truth before him. I remember feeling older than him. I even shamed him for still believing in the story. We are shamed for believing in magic. Once we get past a certain age, it's unrealistic and childish to still believe. At some point, if someone is still talking about Santa, they get sent to the psychiatrist and put on medication for having delusional thoughts. Who are the crazy ones, I wonder?

I've now created a life where it is easy to be me. My work doesn't involve being anything other than me. My relationship fully honours me in all shades, colours, and forms. I have learned to become unapologetically wild. Sometimes, this has meant killing the good girl inside. Sometimes, this has meant blowing up my life and re-experiencing my power. I've learnt to walk in darkness, without running toward the light. I've embraced the beauty and edges of my darkness. I've befriended darkness, but that doesn't mean there isn't doubt and shadows. I've worked through a lot of the limitations that have kept me from being me. The mind is always looking for ways to pull me off of my path and bring me back to a story that disempowers me. That is ancestral. That is collective. That is human. My mind has lured me into caves with men because of what I've experienced. For many lifetimes, I've found my worth and my power in men's eyes and their desire for me. I have been used, abused, and manipulated by men. And that is what I have been clearing in this lifetime. They have also loved and honoured me.

Life is meant to be bumpy. I can't build a fire by meditating and praying for it to appear. I need to rub two sticks together, and as I do this, I am going to sweat and perhaps get frustrated with myself. The friction from the sticks might form painful blisters on my hands. I might even throw the sticks into the air and yell. I might jump up and down, kicking and screaming, moving the anger that burrows deep within my heart. But despite the tumult, I am warm. Suddenly, I feel a release. This is the fire that I am building. This is the fire that I asked for. When we work with the elements and recognise their existence within us, we can move at the pace of the divine mother. When we connect to our inner wildness, we connect to our sisters like Angrboda, who encourage us to hold our ground and stand in our power. She speaks and guides us.

The paths most used are the ones with the biggest boulders and tire marks. A life well lived will show signs of life. When we age, our experiences and our wisdom begin to tattoo themselves onto our physical form, like a beautifully designed map of adventure. Even the best of roads need repair. Life imprints itself on us. We are not meant to be unmarked. Our bodies are created to wear and tear. When we try to resist the touch of life, we remove ourselves from that intimacy with life and step deeper into the illusion that death and aging is a choice. Our hearts will beat slower, and one day our breath will cease. There is beauty in this, and the more that we allow ourselves to dance with this notion, the more we will witness the hand that we've had in everything that occurs. We make a difference here on this earth. Some days will feel void of the divine touch, and others will be filled with magic. We have shadowy parts in us. Parts that we have been trained to dislike and disown. Parts that make us cringe and question our integrity. Parts that have us bow our head and hide. These dark parts of us are also our power. Do not hide from them, and do not hide them from others. They are actually points of connection with others, tools that will deepen our understanding of each other. We are not all light; no one is. It is the melding of dark and light that makes us whole.

The first night that I arrived in Sedona for the rune workshop with Ingrid Kincaid, I left the house I was staying at to grab food down the road. The sun had set about an hour ago and the majestic red mountains were out of sight. My eyes tightened as they searched for something to see in the abyss around me. I pushed my arms out in front of me, attempting to avoid any collisions as I reached into my jean pocket to grab my phone. As I was about to illuminate my flashlight, a thought popped into my head: "I don't need the light to see." I returned my phone into my pocket, took a deep breath, and asked my eyes to see. Instead of feeling fear and trepidation, I felt excitement and peace. I was alone in the darkness on the street in Sedona, and I felt completely at home.

When we rely on the light to see, we miss things. Darkness brings us into the depths of truth. Darkness invites us into the cave of memories where we can uncover what is missing from the surface. Denying our darkness is like pretending that the ocean is only its surface. It would be like looking at the ocean and never knowing about what existed beneath the still waters. My curiosity of the dark mirrors my intrigue of the ocean, a place that is always in existence that we know very little about. To this day, people are discovering languages, information, and societies that have remained unknown for thousands of years because they have been hidden deep in the shadows of caves and caverns. When we work with our intuition and our psychic senses to perceive what is beyond our eye, we uncover deeper layers of every reality. Everything that is "hiding" is in the dark, disguised from the light. Whenever we go through a period of darkness individually or collectively, we emerge with more than we entered. When we are willing to look beyond the surface of what we are being told and dive deep into our own experience, we will recover transformational truths about who we are. We have been taught to fear these parts of ourselves, to bring light into these spaces without question. I am asking you to walk into the darkness without the light and spend some time there uncovering what or who you might've left behind. Chances are, you will find magic.

"My name is Chloe, and I am sovereign. I stand in the center of my circle—ready and open. I am she who walks with the wolves in the darkness and knows her way through. I am she who runs with the wild horses, undomesticated, fierce, and free. I am she who sees in the dark. I am she who sees with her eyes closed."

What lives in you that you are scared of?

When you travel to the depths of your being, descending down into the darkness, as Inanna did, how do you feel? Where do you go?

Can you stand steady and strong, or do you lose your balance?

What happens when you stand in the center of your circle and claim your sovereignty?

Do you hold your staff, steady, or do you drop it?

When you think of the women and men who have raised you and taught you, the elders, do you respect them?

When you receive the call of your ancestors, do you listen?

Do you follow or do you lead?

When darkness envelops the sky and the sun departs, how do you welcome it?

CHAPTER 22

THE HARDEST TRUTH

"How strange that the nature of life is change, yet the nature of human beings is to resist change. And how ironic that the difficult times we fear might ruin us are the very ones that can break us open and help us blossom into who we are meant to be."

– ELIZABETH LESSER

Darkness is our most powerful teacher. It commands our presence. It's in the times of darkness when we really meet ourselves. Everytime we meet darkness again, we wander into a deeper corner of our inner landscape, and we stretch. Our bandwidth grows and the amount that we can hold, be with, and live expands. When we stretch, our magic heightens. When I first started writing this book two years ago when I first moved to Austin, I knew the writing process would end alongside an actual ending in my life. At the time, I felt the ending might be reflected in my marriage. I was at a point of contraction; I questioned everything and felt deeply disconnected from my union with Faris. I never in my wildest dreams would've thought that the ending would be with my wolfdog, Blue.

Our last week with Blue was filled with signs and messages. He was clearly speaking to me and it wasn't until after he left that I began to connect the dots. Exactly one week before he left, we had an attempted intruder come to our house early Saturday morning. If it wasn't for Blue, it could've been bad. Blue startled me awake at 5:30 a.m. on Saturday morning, howling and barking at an alarmingly high pitch. I ran out of the bedroom and saw a large silhouette of a man standing at our back porch right outside our sliding glass doors. The moment I turned on our porch lights, he started to quickly shuffle out our gates and down the street. I grabbed Blue from his crate, and he bolted out the doors, nose to the ground, following the stranger's scent. With Blue by my side, I felt safe and strong enough to go after the intruder. We felt like an impenetrable team. I knew that Blue would protect me. In the soul journeys that I did with Blue, he showed me the lifetimes that we have lived together, prior to this one. He showed himself as a wolf, my wolf and guardian. He showed us living lifetimes together, just us. This intruder experience created an even deeper appreciation for Blue. He had an instinctual desire to protect me and only me, so much so that he became dangerous. It was as if he was too much for this body and this life. He was too much of a wolf for a dog. He was the largest australian shepherd I had ever seen or heard of, 75 pounds in weight.

The last few weeks with Blue were hazed over by a sleepless fog. My mind was preparing me for the nightmare to come, disguising my fear with unlimited amounts of adrenaline. Exactly one month before he died, Blue attacked our other dog, Ollie. The day that he attacked him, I performed my first moon cycle ritual, pouring my menstrual blood that I collected over the four days, onto our yard, releasing my divine womb codes into the earth. That night Blue attacked Ollie, puncturing his left shoulder blade with his unforgiving canine fangs. It wasn't the first time he had attacked Ollie, but it was the first time he had shed blood. I quickly grabbed Ollie, cradling him in my arms. When he hopped onto the floor, my forearms were left painted in thick streaks of blood. The moment I saw the blood, I thought of my womb ceremony. In some unexplainable way, it felt connected. That month we kept the dogs separated. Anytime Blue heard or saw Ollie, he attempted to attack him. Ollie was no longer safe in our home.

Three days before he died, Blue was sleeping on the cold concrete floor of our bedroom while I was asleep in bed. As he always would, Faris came to grab Blue and move him into his crate. The moment Faris reached down to pet Blue on his fluffy head, Blue jolted up onto all fours and growled low and slow. Faris backed off and gave him some space, unsure of how to respond to this new and unexpected behaviour. I woke up to the energy change in the room and looked at Blue as his behaviour shifted. Since I was a little girl, I always knew right before an animal was going to react. Something in my blood responded, as if from memory. Seeing and feeling what was going to happen before it did. Blue lunged forward, barking and growling at Faris. The look in his eyes changed as if the Blue that we knew had left his body. For some reason, he wanted to hurt Faris. I jumped out of bed and grabbed Blue's back legs to pull him away from Faris. Somehow I knew that Blue wouldn't hurt me like he would Faris in this moment. Somehow, I always knew. Blue did bite me, and he left a colourful bruise. It wasn't the first bite that I got from Blue. Since he was a puppy, I got many bruises. Blue always had the chance to inflict major damage, but his bites were always more of a warning. He broke skin, but I knew that he was trying to hold back. He was fighting his mind. The next night, it happened again, except this time I couldn't deny it. Faris no longer felt safe in our home. His dog had turned on him. That night, I brought Blue into the bathroom with me while I showered as I always did. This time, it felt different. Instead of taking a nap and waiting for my wet limbs to emerge for him to lick the water off of, he squished himself up in the corner and his aura felt grey and foggy. When I stepped out of the shower, he dropped his head down as if to warn me of something. I got the message: if I came any closer, he would hurt me too.

The week that Blue entered our lives, he came with clear signs. The first time I saw his photo, I heard the lyrics of "Hey Jude" by the Beatles playing with "Blue" replacing "Jude." When I first saw the picture of him, I heard a voice in my head clearly say, "Hi, my name is Blue and I'm yours." When we visited the farm to meet Blue when he was a puppy, we met his Mum, Juniper. She had a moment with both Faris and I and gave us her blessing, staring deep into our eyes. The day of the intruder, the week before Blue left, I was in the bath and Blue sat outside the shower doors as he always did. As he looked at me through the glass doors, the song "Hey Jude" appeared in my mind again for the first time since we first met 15 months ago. I was curious about the significance, but the adrenaline in my mind protected me from truly knowing why that happened. When Blue first showed himself to me through a picture on google, I worried that Faris wouldn't accept him.

I connected to Blue' spirit and asked him to make it really obvious that he was showing up for us to adopt him into our family. I told Faris to look out for signs. That day was covered in Blue. Everything was the colour blue. Every dog that Faris met was named Blue. While we were stopped at a red light, a man crossed the street and was decked out in blue. He was wearing bright royal blue shoes, baby blue headphones, a blue shirt, and a cobalt blue backpack. It was so obvious, even Faris couldn't deny it.

Blue was with us for 15 months, and it felt like 15 years. He was the dog I had always dreamt of having and the wolf that I wished for. He came and went like a spontaneous blue flame. I always said that he was true to his earth sign, virgo. He was powerful and wasn't going to stand for anything that was hiding under the surface. He entered our world like a fast and fiery comet without much warning. Blue brought us together and helped to heal our family. He was the ultimate teacher for Faris, Ollie, and I. His beauty was prince-like. In the year that he was with us, he transformed everything for us. He taught Ollie how to be with other dogs and how to share. He taught Faris and I how to really love each other and be a team. He invited Faris into the masculine and empowered him. He brought me to the runes and my Nordic ancestry, connecting me to my inner wild. I now wonder if he was the wolf that I saw on that morning driving through the rockies.

In Nordic mythology, the creation story tells the tale of how everything came into life in the space between fire and ice. Between the Southern realm of heat and the Northern realm of cold, a running thawed fluid birthed the frost giant Ymir who later fed from a cow called Audhumla (who is known as the mother). Audhumla began to lick salty ice blocks, and after a few days, a man was born. The story continues with more births, and some deaths and the world as we know it now began to form. The interesting creation story is rooted in the notion that chaos creates life and without contrast and duality, life ends. This powerful theme weaves its way through Nordic mythology and the whispers of the runes. It is shown to us everyday in nature. Life is meant to be messy and, at times, chaotic. When we judge the chaos as bad or wrong, and we attach ourselves and our expectations to it, we dismiss its offerings. Our time with Blue wasn't what we expected or wanted, but it was what we needed. It brought a lot of chaos into our lives, and it forced us to make a choice that would bring us back into balance. It was our choice to make, and no one could make it for us.

Saying goodbye to Blue's physical form and making the choice to kill him was the hardest decision of my life. I use the word "kill" because it is the truth, the hardest and most compassionate truth. I did what he asked me to do and what I knew I had to do. I did the thing that felt impossible, what I feared the most. Before it came into my knowing, it was never an option. It was an action that I previously judged others for. And until it strangely felt right, it felt incredibly wrong. Every part of me wanted to keep fighting for him. To keep trying to support him and create a sliver of harmony in our lives. For months, I agonised over every possible option, even entertaining the idea of leaving Ollie with Faris and buying property in the country to live just Blue and I, wolf and woman. From the moment we got Blue, I felt that something was off. He was the rebel in puppy class and the trainers asked us to pick him up and hold him in time outs constantly. He always took things too far, and had a bit of an attitude that felt more than just puppy aggression. He picked his first big fight with another dog when he was 4 months in our apartment complex dog park, and from that moment, he felt like a ticking time bomb. We never knew when he was going to snap at another dog. It became impossible to take him out, without running into another dog in the stairwell which never ended well. So we bought a house with a big yard. We worked with four different trainers, and they all arrived at the same devastating conclusion. We called every shelter and rescue in Texas and the surrounding areas, and reached back out to the breeder. I booked sessions with every animal communicator and medium that I could find. Those last 3 months every thought and conversation that I had was around Blue and getting help. And until he attacked Faris, after attacking Ollie, euthanasia was completely out of the question. Even once the idea popped into my mind, I shamed myself for thinking about it and kept going. And then the last trainer we worked with, who ended up being the most helpful, informative and compassionate of all of the trainers, had the courage to call me at 11pm and tell me that her professional opinion was to euthanize Blue for behaviour. She voiced her concern and validated my fear, that if we didn't do it, someone else who didn't know him and possibly didn't love him, would do it anyways. She told me that even though it seemed like the most horrible choice, it could be the most loving for Blue. I'll never forget that conversation, and I'll always be grateful that this trainer had enough courage and compassion to tell me the truth. Up until that moment, it seemed like every other professional we had spoken to danced around it, without actually owning it.

The morning that he was euthanised, I woke up in tears. I knew what was coming before it came. I spent those early hours with him, just Blue and I. We sat in the dark, cuddling and talking. He lay by my side, grinding his teeth on his bone, momentarily pausing to look into my eyes. His amber eyes always penetrated my heart. Although I felt safe with him, I could sense that there was something different building inside of him. I could feel him fighting it. A few hours into our time together, the energy in Blue once again shifted. He pulled back from me, tucked his lips and quietly growled. His eyes revealed an unpredictable energy that I had always felt in him but it was deeply hidden. I knew that he was warning me. I gave him his space and told him that he was safe. This was the first time that I was truly scared of what Blue might do next. I was the last one left that he hadn't attacked. Despite the many times that he had bit me, I always knew that I was safe with him. This time was different. It wasn't Blue. His aggression was escalating by the minute. He was ready to go, to leave the limitations and conflict of his physical form. His work was done. Faris wasn't able to be in the room when Blue left. The sight or sound of him or Ollie triggered Blue into an unbearable rage. It was just Blue and I, similar to how our journey started. The moment the solution entered his blood stream, his eyes moved in a strange direction, and the vet mentioned the likelihood that he had been dealing with something mentally. Two weeks prior, during a session with an animal communicator, she had told me that Blue had head trauma that was likely from being dropped as a young puppy, before we got him. Even though these assessments confirmed a sense that I always had, they did nothing to soothe the onslaught of grief that I felt had been injected into my bloodstream. As soon as I returned home and felt the foreign emptiness of his absence, I wanted to rush back to the vet and ask them to bring him back, to reverse my choice. As grief goes, the shock of his physical disappearance was an unwelcome nuance that I had to gradually and gently adjust to.

Before Blue died, I called in support from every direction. My heart needed to know that I did everything I could to help him. One of the angels who showed up is a healer in Canada who works with animals of all shapes and sizes including horses and elephants. I brought Blue into my office with me and we began the session together. I wanted to ask Blue, through Loesje, why he started to attack Ollie.

"This might come out quite harsh, but Blue is telling me that Ollie smells like death, and he is trying to help him out, by killing him." Loesje's words shot directly into my lungs, emptying out the air. I breathed in, looking into Blue's emerald eyes as he stared directly into mine, sitting in front me like a trusted direwolf, dripping saliva onto my thighs. "Blue keeps showing me Ollie's mouth and that his breath smells really bad. Have you had Ollie's teeth checked recently?" As Loesje spoke these words, I felt them reflect the arbitrary thoughts I had been noticing in my head over the past few weeks. I too had wondered if something was going on with Ollie, specifically in his mouth. "This is what happens sometimes in the wild, when one of the pack members is weak. In fact, in the wild, they often do kill pack members when they know that they are ill or weakened. It is partly a survival mechanism of protecting the others and not being slowed down, and it is also, I feel, a beautiful aspect of the wild. Animals don't see death the way that humans do. They don't hold onto suffering as we do." I sat there with Blue in my office, absorbing Loesje's words and feeling both fear and truth dance inside of me like a pair of mismatched tango partners. Everything she said was what I knew and believed, but there's a difference between knowing something, and acting on it.

Loesje was one of the many animal psychics and communicators that I spoke with before making the choice to euthanize Blue. When Loesje asked Blue why he was attacking Ollie, that was one of his responses. He also showed her through psychic vision, that he experienced head trauma as a puppy (most likely from being dropped by one of the breeder's children before we got him), and that he felt stuck in his current physical body. It's how I always felt; that Blue was too wild for this body and this life. Almost as if he was repeating another lifetime we had lived together where he was my fierce dire wolf, and would do anything, even kill, to keep me safe. During that session, Blue's wild self really came out. As Loesje was running a few energy healing programs through his system, he almost ripped open my couch in what looked like a frenzy. He bounced around my office like a ping pong ball, knocking over anything and everything that he touched, including my water glass. He even somehow ripped off his collar. It wasn't anything like the 'zoomies' that you see in puppies. It was angry and wild. After working with Loesje, we also met with a few other experts and trainers. As the weeks went by, instead of getting better, things just worsened, until Blue ended up attacking Faris.

Blue's first response about Ollie never left me, and the day after Blue died, over a month after that call with Loesje, I took Ollie to the vet to get his teeth checked, even though the idea of returning to the scene of Blue's death the day after felt impossible. Even though I felt there was a lot more to it for Blue, a part of me also felt that he was onto something with Ollie's health. The vet looked at his teeth, and he came back with a full bill of good health with the simple recommendation to get a teeth cleaning in 3-4 months. I accepted her assessment, took Ollie home, and I considered myself extremely lucky to still have Ollie in my life.

The next 3 months were filled with bundles of gratitude for Ollie. I would say that for those 3 months, Ollie didn't walk much. He was in my arms as much as he could be. He also began to follow me around like he did as a puppy. He began to do things that he hadn't done in years, as if with Blue gone he felt the need to really show up for me again. Once again, he was my main guardian. In so many ways, Ollie carried us through the grief of Blue. The irony is that one of the reasons I felt called to get Blue, was to soften the transition of when Ollie eventually died. I never in a million years thought that Blue would be the one dying, and Ollie would be there to hold me through it. Once again, he came everywhere with us. With Blue gone, we began to realise how easy of a dog Ollie always was. One of Blue's many gifts was that he allowed us to truly appreciate Ollie.

Since Blue left, I see him everywhere. Suddenly, everything is blue again: street signs, candle ingredients, building names, dreams, and conversations. Blue died on December 18th, 2020. When I think of him, I see a red cardinal dancing along our fence line, reflecting Blue's foxy red fur. Two days after he left his body, my aunt in Wales visited his spirit during a shamanic journey. Her description of him reflected the way that I saw him, running free and wild in the mountains. She said that he was surrounded by unconditional love and the great horned Celtic god, Cernunnos, the lord of the wild things.

The wild ride of grief has been one I've never experienced this consciously before. When a loved one leaves the physical realm, they leave behind a thick fog of memories of how they touched our daily lives. The streaks of his hot slobber still sit on my office windows, marking where he'd sit and watch the world daily as I worked. Every time I use the ice machine, a sharp wave of heat hit my heart. Blue loved ice, and everytime he heard the ice machine, he came running eager to get some slippery cubes to play with. Anytime I clean our lounge upstairs and fluff the pillows, I turn the one pillow that he ripped apart and expose the black cotton surgical stitches. The day after he left, it rained all day, washing away his physical remnants in our backyard. It felt strange for Blue to be gone, but his bite marks still live on my arm. Every morning I'd glance down at my right forearm to see the bruises change colours and the cuts scabbing over. I strangely want them to leave scars, to leave his marks. My mind doesn't want to forget him and my heart never will. Grief takes you on a deep and revealing journey through darkness. When someone dies, we are forced to face the limitations of the physical world. We are confronted with the ultimate truth that the physical form dies and that death is inevitable. Everything dies. There is so much shame, denial, and repression associated with death. I am starting to understand why Blue chose this path with me. It can be a lonely road to euthanize your young dog for aggression. Choosing death can be a road that others judge without having walked it. It is a revealing road, and it helps us to meet our relationship with death. When is it okay to die? When is it not okay to die? I know that keeping Blue alive and continuing to try new methods would've been more about me than Blue. Making the impossible decision to say goodbye to him was a gift to him. Forcing him to stay would've been a selfish choice. And it takes something to recognise that. It takes a deep truth that comes from standing in the center of my circle and befriending the dark.

A saving grace has been a Facebook support group that our trainer suggested for people who have had to euthanize their dogs for aggression. This safe space has allowed me the opportunity to find myself in other's familiar stories and massage out any guilt or shame that I carry beneath the surface for the unimaginable choice we all had to make. What struck me most is the level of unconditional love that each person offered to every story that was shared. No matter the circumstances, instead of responding with judgment, questions, and offense, the resounding response was support. As the weeks passed, reading other people's stories, I realised how much shame people hold over themselves and the fear of what others will think. At times, this Facebook support group felt like a dark hidden cave that provided us with the shelter we craved after such traumatising experiences. Witnessing this shook me because one of my fears was how others would respond to what happened. It's that same fear that appears when we share our most vulnerable truth. The truth that we keep locked in the shadows of our mind: the things we've done and desired. We fear the truth will deem us unlovable. The irony about grief is how alone you feel in grief, even though it is the most shared experience for all humans.

However sad, there is release in death. Before death, we are waiting. Even though I didn't want to acknowledge it, I was waiting for change. I knew that I wouldn't be able to continue living the way that we were for much longer. The heightened energy of resistance in our house was loud. When Blue left his physical form, the room filled with peace and stillness. When we returned home, everything was quiet. The next morning, the house was irrevocably peaceful. We didn't want to admit it, but we felt relieved. Something had been released.

In Sedona, Ingrid talked a lot about what happens when we hold onto things that are ready to go. When we ignore the call for change, because of our fear or attachments. Fehu is a rune that really speaks to this energy. Fehu says that whatever we aren't using is using us. Everything is energy, and everything involves an energy exchange. To practice and embody this, we have to have a relationship with the dark and the light, because sometimes that change requires action and stepping outside of our comfort zones. Sometimes, it's an easy process of letting go that happens seamlessly. And sometimes, it involves more friction and confrontation. When we bought our house in Austin, we no longer had a kitchen island and so we didn't need our beautiful bar stools anymore. I loved our bar stools. They were a unique horseradish mustard colour, and the bases formed an eclectic geometric shape that really fit in with my style. As a puppy, Blue loved to sleep directly on top of the legs and as he grew, he continued to contort his body to fit under the stools. There was something about them that he loved. I tried my best to make use of them in our new home, but the truth is that they didn't fit. We explored the idea of building a coffee bar at our front door, but the bar would be just a bit too high for the stools. You'd be reaching awkwardly for your coffee. I asked Faris to use one of the stools as his office chair, but he rarely used it because he had a standing desk. One of the stools sat in our back closet under the stairs, holding things. When Blue died, I felt the push to put them on Facebook Marketplace. I priced them relatively high; a sign that I wasn't really ready to let go of them. Some people made offers, but I turned them all down. I wasn't ready. They remained standing and taking up space for a few more weeks. We made the decision to scatter Blue's ashes in our back yard and at a magical spot on one of our favourite hikes that we would take Blue and Ollie. I realised that keeping his ashes stuck in a box didn't feel right. I remembered what Ingrid had said, "don't let your possessions possess you". Even though I liked the idea of holding onto a piece of him, I knew it wasn't right. We needed to return all of him to the earth. Scattering his ashes onto the earth was a joyous experience. We cried, laughed and danced with him. It wasn't heavy, like I thought it might be. I realised that I needed to rearrange our living room, now that the credenza wasn't holding his urn. Once I moved things around, I also felt like I needed to wash the floors, and do a big clearing of our entire house, back to front. I used chinese floor wash, lit incense, opened the doors and really enjoyed this ritual. I felt Blue with me, following me around and enjoying it as much as I was. That night, I received three messages on Facebook Marketplace for the bar stools. There was something about one of the ladies that drew me in. It felt like she was meant to have them. She agreed with my price, and they decided to come that night to pick them up. She said that her and her husband had just moved to Austin, and her favourite colour was yellow. I spent some time with the stools, blessing and clearing them and saying goodbye. When they arrived, she shared that they moved here from Vancouver, and they met in Dubai, which perfectly mirrored my journey. The stools were going to their new home, and it ended up requiring very little effort. It was time, and even though I was very sad to let go of them and their memories, I also felt a spacious release.

We can't box light in the good and dark in the bad. And just because we speak about the dark as its own being, doesn't mean we need to then demonise the light. I see myself as a lightworker and a darkworker; I can travel to both sides and edges without losing myself. That's a large part of what my journey has taught me. I know how to walk in the light, and I know how to walk in the dark. This is something that many of us have forgotten and lost, in the same way that we've forgotten who we are and where we come from. If we choose to stay isolated on one side, we create an imbalance. The light is its own being, and the dark is too. Sometimes they work together, and when they do it provides a powerful and revealing contrast. But it's important we can also see them as their own, just like day and night are not the same. They each have unique offerings. When I look back at my time with Blue, the whole experience is rounded by the dark and the light moments. They taught me so much and they were both a part of Blue. He was sweet, loving, playful and beautiful, and he was also harsh, stubborn and wild. To only remember the light parts of him would be a lie. Sometimes, when I'm feeling low and I'm letting my mind feed the guilt, I follow that lie. I remember him as a puppy and how amazing it felt to be his mother. When I recenter myself, and I invoke the wild woman in me, I remember that he also did things that weren't acceptable and that couldn't be left without action. Remembering both sides doesn't mean that I didn't love him unconditionally, it means that I was willing to travel to the edges with him.

It's impossible to know how everything is going to go. We are not here to control what life brings us, or to perfectly plan for it. The dark is such a generous life partner because it is guaranteed to bring us an abundance of growth. It is the true catalyst to creation. It is through befriending the dark that we allow the light in. The expansive quality of life allows us to stand in something as deep and dark as grief and still feel the sparks of divinity dance among us. The dark is an intimate space. It is not evil. It is divine, and it is not conquered. Don't deny its presence or ignore it when it is knocking on your door. Invite it into the silence and listen for the wisdom it brings with it.

Have you ever had to make a choice that didn't make sense?

Have you ever had to make a choice that felt impossible, and right?

When is the right time to die?

What is your relationship to death?

How do you feel about death?

What are your beliefs around death?

CHAPTER 23

BEFRIENDING DEATH

"To go in the dark with a light, is to know the light.
To know the dark, go dark.
Go without sight, and find that the dark, too, blooms and sings,
and is traveled by dark feet, and dark wings."
- WENDELL BERRY

We pile into the car after saying goodbye to my mum at the ranch. It was the end of another summer season. The sun had barely risen and the hills were covered in a thick morning fog. Ollie propped himself up on Sam's lap, said farewell to the ranch, and took his last breaths of his favourite place. The car felt sad.

Different than usual, my sister-in-law, Tori, began the drive and I was in the back seat, sitting in the darkness. I knew this drive like the back of my hand, and my favourite way to enjoy it was solo, just Ollie and I. We had just left the ranch when suddenly I jumped out of my seat, reaching forward and yelling at Tori to slow down. Within eyesight, I caught a scene I had never seen before: a massive bald eagle was flying full speed ahead darting toward the ground, and it was surrounded by a circle of ravens. This unlikely sight was puzzling, and it took a long moment to understand what was happening. The ravens were hunting the eagle, swarming around it in a cloud of darkness. Tori stomped on the brakes as the birds flew directly over the bonnet of our car and disappeared into the fog. My eyes blinked, attempting to recalibrate to the reality that they just witnessed. Tears poured down my cheeks, and the heat of my body sank into the seat. Something about this moment felt like it was for me, despite my brother telling me it was random and a coincidence as he usually did. I couldn't deny how I felt as I watched the ravens envelop the eagle in darkness. Every time I drive from the ranch back to Vancouver, I feel deeply connected to the animals and the energy of the land. This moment moved me more than ever before. Just like when I saw the wolf. Surrounded by the ravens, the eagle was being chased by darkness, windborne like a flying arrow.

. . . .

After Blue died, I felt like darkness was chasing me, the darkness of grief, shame, guilt, and judgment. I was the one who called the vet and made the appointment, and I was the only one in the room when he left. A month after he left, a dark wave of grief enveloped me as my womb bled. The numbing shock had worn off, and my body released the largest dose of pain into my bloodstream. As my body shed the blood of the past, I wailed. I sat on the tiled floor of our shower, waiting for the running water to wash away the crippling pain. My eyes still look for Blue. My mind tormented me with stories, memories, and thoughts. Questions that I couldn't answer which left me in a state of intense self-betrayal and debilitating shame. What if I made a mistake? What if I waited? I could've done something different: a different trainer, a different day, something different. The pain of my thoughts were agonising and no matter where I went or what I did, they were right behind me, surrounding me like a pack of ravens hunting me. I couldn't distract myself from it, or fly in another direction.

My aunt suggested that it was time for me to do a shamanic journey to connect with my animal guide and possibly meet Blue. During that journey, I met a beautiful vulture. She was huge and felt like a cross between a fiery dragon and a magical phoenix. Her wing span seemed larger than my own, decorated in brown, black, white, and golden feathers. I heard the words, "bearded vulture" and realised that this was a rare and ancient vulture who was known to eat the bones of the deceased. My mind wanted Blue, or his wolf soul to meet me, but here was a vulture greeting me. Her power was undeniable, standing at the entrance of the cave, ready to guide me. When I returned from the journey, I realised that I had begun to connect to vultures since moving to Austin. I see them everywhere, and have at times wondered if they were the great condor. I had never seen a vulture in the wild before, apart from on an African safari. I had always seen vultures as bad and evil, symbols of death, scavengers, and bad omens. My relationship with death was changing though. My relationship with the dark had changed, and the vulture reminded me to look at death differently. Death and life are partners, and sometimes in order to create life we must destroy life. Since Blue died, I've found myself noticing how many dogs in the city seem stuck. We sometimes forget that dogs are animals, descendents of the wolf, and that they are wild. We try to get them to do what we want them to do and to live our lives, but they are and always will be wild. In some ways, we take away our pets' freedom. We remove the opportunity for choice. When the grief allowed me to see through the heaviness, I was reminded of similar thoughts that I had before Blue was born. How gates, fences, crates, kennels, leashes, and collars in some way are forms of control and entrapment, trying to control the untamable. We cage them, trap them, break them, and force them to behave in ways that is not their nature. We remove them from nature. We breed them to become more of what we want them to be or look like. Remembering the way of an anthropologist to observe behaviour without judgment, I thought about some of the strange things that we do to contain the wild in our own homes. I thought of some of the wolves that we met at a Wolf Sanctuary here in Texas, who were rescued from homes that tried to keep them as pets. Perhaps Blue was reminding me that the wild lives in all of our blood and that the laws and cycles of nature are inescapable and uncontrollable.

Seeing my vulture guide reminded me of the story my aunt Ananda told me about the young Tibetan girl, when I was a little girl. I thought of Blue and the power of his soul. He came here, in this lifetime, for transformation. His birth date was 9/9/19, a true virgo representing the force of earth energy. I felt his power the day I met him. The purity of his soul was reflected in what he was willing to do and undergo. He was willing to be judged as uncontrollable, aggressive, and dominant and to hold that shame energy so that I could see beyond those judgments and feel something different. In my life, he brought both love and fear, perfection and shame, beauty and destruction, silence and chaos. He felt like an angel, a messenger, somehow teaching me to look beyond the surface experience and reach deep into the roots of the earth to understand life differently and increase my capacity of what I could hold and be with. I had to step further outside of the story of losing my dog, making a wrong decision, or being a bad dog mum to understand and feel the offering that his life provided.

That weekend Faris, Ollie, and I decided to retreat to a cabin in hill country to get away from the noise of the city and our grief. As we drove along the bumpy, dirt country road towards the entrance, three vultures flew over our car and planted themselves on a large tree beside the front gate to the property. I chose not to read into it too much, knowing that vultures were prolific in the area. On the morning that we left, two days later Faris pointed out the window, signaling their presence. There they were, all three vultures, sitting in the tree. Their presence and positioning was undeniable.

Vultures and death continued to grace my path. A week after the cabin, I was driving home and saw three big black birds surrounding a dead animal on the side of the road. I intended to keep driving, but my hands turned the wheel to go back. I pulled over and stepped out of the car. Three large vultures stood before me eating death. I stood there with them, watching them for several minutes. Instead of squirming or feeling sick, I felt intrigued and curious. I felt honoured and in awe of these three dark beings. There was nothing evil about them. They were honouring the body of a possum who had likely been killed by a car. They stood around its dead body in a circle. It was beautiful. It was life being fed by death. It felt as if they were sharing death with me, assuring me that Blue's death was taken care of.

Seeing the vultures and the possum reminded me of another story I had once read in Ted Andrews book, Animal Speak. It was a story about a time when the sun lived very close to the earth, and life on earth was becoming impossible. The animal world gathered to create a change. Of these animals, there was a possum who volunteered to wrap his tail around the sun and begin running towards the heavens to pull it further away from the earth. As he went, the sun got too hot and burnt his tail. As the story goes, this is now why possums have hairless tails. The final animal to be presented by Andrews was the vulture. At the time, the vulture had a full head of remarkable feathers. The vulture knew that if it didn't volunteer its power, the earth would soon burn into ash. It placed its head against the sun and flew towards the heavens, pushing it with unexplainable force. Although it felt the burning heat of the sun damaging and destroying its feathers, it continued to fly away from the earth until the sun was a safe distance away. The vulture lost the rich feathers on its head, balding itself for life.

It was up to me to choose what I believed about witnessing the vultures. I could deny the magic and pretend that it didn't mean anything to me, but I knew that it did. Just like I knew, deep down that Blue was ready to go. I could stay in a place of seeing these expressions of life as dark and evil and something to fear, or I could witness the beauty and necessity of their roles in the cycle. It was also up to me what I chose to believe about Blue's life and death. There is an undefinable difference between what we want to know and what we actually know. And it takes something to hold steady in your intuitive belief when your mind and fear want nothing to do with it. I was reminded of the time I spent at the ranch, four years ago, just Ollie, me and the elders. I was reminded of how I knew I needed to stay no matter what, despite how much I wanted to leave everyday when the night arrived. To move through my fear and realise that their presence was nothing to be afraid of. The limitations of judgment keep us from honouring our deepest truth. When we catch ourselves in the constraints of "right" and "wrong," we cut ourselves off from the wisdom that we all have access to. Judgment disconnects us from each other and hinders the healing that is required. Our minds love to talk us out of anything intuitive or magical. It's up to us to choose something different. It's up to us to choose our truth. I couldn't fix what happened. I couldn't make it go away or do something to make it better. I had to embody the wisdom of the wild mother: Berkana, the rune who both creates and destroys. I had to surrender to the mess that I felt and allow the arrow's tip to puncture my heart. I had to trust my choice. I had to trust Blue. I had to trust my intuition.

. . . .

One night, three months after Blue's death, we were watching Aladdin upstairs in our tv lounge and I noticed that Ollie wasn't with us. Somehow, while our eyes were glued to the large screen, he made his way downstairs. Feeling the oddness of this, I went looking for him and found him alone in the dark in our bedroom. Intuitively, I immediately knew that something was wrong, and I felt guided to check the inside of his mouth. There, at the top of his right K9, was a red lump on his gums. I wished I didn't feel what I felt, but what I felt was dread. I immediately remembered what Loesje, the animal communicator, had told me during the healing session I did with her for Blue, four months earlier. I remembered that Blue told her that Ollie smelled like death. I sat with Ollie for a few minutes, looking into his chocolate diamond eyes. I felt the wind shifting outside, as we sat there together in the darkness, listening to the silence that so often precedes change.

We immediately booked an appointment at the vet, and within a few days, we were waiting for the results of the biopsy. Our vet was hopeful, but told us, based on his preliminary assessment of the cells, that it quite possibly could be oral malignant melanoma. The biopsy results took over a week, and during that time, the mass in his mouth was impatiently growing. Death was coming. I felt it. I knew it. As we waited, I called on all of my magic. I lit spell candles, did a protection spell, and cleared his body and the space everyday. Any chance that I got, I offered Ollie reiki. We got the biopsy results 9 days after that vet visit, and they confirmed the inevitable. Ollie had oral malignant melanoma, and it was aggressive.

I knew that I would be saying goodbye to my sweet boy sooner than we were told and much sooner than Faris expected. The vet told us that we might have 60 days if we took the palliative care route. He suggested that we meet with the animal oncologist to assess our options. Having gone through the death initiation with Blue, I knew what it felt like this time when death was knocking and I was resisting. Once again, I saw myself sitting at a crossroads, holding my dog's life in my hands. I knew that I would be the one that would have to make the choice, and it wouldn't be made for me. I knew that part of the responsibility of taking away Ollie's freedom, would be giving it back to him, even if I wasn't ready to let him go.

The morning that we took Ollie to the oncologist, he seemed really depressed. He didn't want to get out of bed, which was rare for him, even with malignant cancer. The night before, he randomly peed in his bed, which is something he hadn't done since he was a puppy. In the back of my mind, I knew that going to the oncologist was just a way to stretch the truth. In ways, it felt like a waste, but I knew it would provide our logical minds with the evidence we wanted to make the choice that we were rejecting. The oncologist gave us more bad news. Ollie's options were slim and anything that they could do, was just about giving us more time with him. It wouldn't be for him; it would be for us to hold onto him. I knew the moment I heard the options, that Ollie wanted no part of it. Ollie didn't want his jaw and nose cut out to remove the tumour, that would just return. Ollie didn't want to visit the oncologist every week for 5-6 weeks to receive radiation therapy, and maybe give him a few more months in this dying body. Ollie was ready to go. I could feel it. That day, once again he peed, this time on our floor pillows in our tv lounge. My logical mind told me that it was a side-effect of the painkillers, but my heart told me it was Ollie getting his message across.

It was interesting to notice how Ollie's demeanour changed when we decided against the oncology options. The next morning we woke up to him bouncing on top of us in bed, barking and singing, like he always had. He had a new boost of energy and he was ready for breakfast. From that point on, he didn't pee inside. The oncologist told us that the palliative care route would probably give us one month with him before things became unbearable. I could feel that things were going to happen much quicker than that. The mass in his mouth continued to grow at an exponential rate. The tissue was beginning to die, and his mouth was filled with black and brown necrotic tissue. His breath reminded me of the stories I had read about Hella, Angrboda's daughter, and her legs with rotting skin. The guardian of the dead. I wondered if Hella was here with us, in the house, waiting to welcome Ollie into her realm of the dead. I started to wince and gag when Ollie gave me kisses. I had to hold my breath when I cuddled him close. Faris and I started to have persistent dull headaches from the smell. His imminent death was inescapable. I could smell it, just like Blue could months prior. I remember watching a movie where dogs were trained to sniff out cancer. I always said that Blue would've made an amazing tracker.

Ollie was on round-the-clock pain killers. He had a massive tumour in his mouth that was getting to him, even if he didn't make it seem like it. Animals have a different relationship to pain than we do. Not only do they have a distinct and tolerant way of being with it, but they also communicate it differently. What I've noticed is that our animals are in our lives for a reason. They have a purpose and they honour their purpose until their last breath. They don't waiver on it or question or doubt it. They know it, and they follow it. Ollie came into my life at a time when I needed a true guardian. He was a Christmas present from my brother and boyfriend at the time, Mark. Finally, after asking for a dog since birth, I had one. And he was a precious tiny ball of black fluff that looked like a little baby bear. Ollie journeyed with me through my twenties, vetted every man who entered my life and traveled by my side as I walked through life.

I was back in the painful space that I had just emerged from, but this time I was there with Ollie. Somehow, I thought that perhaps Ollie would live forever. After being with me for over thirteen years, I suppose I got used to him being there. He never had any health issues and was the most energetic, active and happy dog I'd ever met. He was down for anything and always ready. And he had cancer. And he was dying. I knew what I had to do. I called a service here in Austin that offered home euthanasia. We were going to make it special for him. We were going to honour him. The more I leaned into embracing his death, the more he came to life. All he wanted to do was run around outside with his ball, and eat everything. Suddenly, all of the house rules around not begging for food or whining outside of my office door while I was in client sessions, flew right out the window. Ollie got to snack on everything we were, and he joined in as many sessions as he could, offering his support and wisdom to my clients.

I had many conversations with Ollie before he died. I let him know that I was ready and that his job in this form was done. We spent so many hours just looking into each other's eyes. I surrounded him and us with as much support and love as possible, which included another amazing animal psychic, Julie whom I had worked with before. Even though I was talking to Ollie everyday, I knew that there were some things that I was missing, in my own human attachment to him.

"He's telling me that he cries at night when you are sleeping. He keeps showing himself crying in the darkness." Julie told me one day as we were chatting about whether or not Ollie was ready to go. Even though I had made the decision, I was having a hard time choosing the right day. Which day is the right day to kill your dog? With Blue, I had less time for this because we weren't safe at home and his aggression was escalating every minute. With Ollie, his death was looming, but in many ways, he seemed okay. If I stuck with my logical mind, I would continue to keep him around, justifying it by the fact that was still eating, drinking water, sleeping, and playing like a wild coyote when we brought his ball out. That day, Ollie followed me around everywhere I went, whining. Whenever I sat down, he would sit right in front of me, staring into my eyes, whining. I scheduled his euthanasia for 2 days from that moment. Later that night, I woke up randomly and realised that Ollie was crying. There, alone in the darkness, he was crying. He was in pain. He was ready. He just didn't want us to see it. He didn't want us to know that he was suffering. That wasn't part of his job.

Ollie left that Wednesday and he had a life celebration to complete it. People came to visit the day before, he did facetime and zoom calls with loved ones and received a lot of messages from the people whose lives he had touched. When it was time for him to go, he fell asleep in my arms while licking as many crumbs as he could of his peanut butter doggy doughnut from my sticky hand. In true Ollie fashion, he left us crying and laughing. He continued to fulfill his role as my guardian, even in his death.

Death is never convenient. There is no 'right' time to choose death. Death asks us to surrender and let go of needing for things to make sense. The moment the vet who would administer the euthanasia for Ollie entered our home that day, she thanked us for making the choice before it was obvious. She told us that sometimes, people wait so long, that the tumour has taken over their dog's face and the smell in the house is intolerable. Hearing this confirmed what I felt, and further fueled my desire to share what I have chosen to share in this book. It made me think about how we don't let people die with honour. Sometimes, we drag life on to the point that death needs to completely take someone over before they are given the permission to leave. Here I was going through the same experience with Ollie, less than 4 months after Blue. Learning the same lesson. Gaining similar wisdom. Death must be honoured, just as life is. Holding onto life is just another way that we attach and try to control the uncontrollable. In efforts to delay our suffering, we create more suffering. Death has so much to teach us.

When Ollie took his last breath, I felt him leave his body. Within a second, his physical form that was filled with so much life and force, was suddenly empty. Suddenly, this beautiful, fluffy black, white and brown body became meaningless, because it was no longer Ollie. Holding onto Ollie's body would be like holding onto the illusion that the physical life is all that there is. Even though both Ollie and Blue's deaths were painful for us. For them, they were peaceful. As my mentor and friend Lynnette said, Ollie saw an exit ramp and he took it. When we were preparing for the vet to arrive, Faris said we should move our car out of the garage, so that she can park in the garage and easily transport Ollie's body without others seeing it. I appreciated the thought of Faris' suggestion and immediately turned it down. It made me think about death in our world and how we hide it. When a human dies, their bodies are usually zipped into a black body bag and very discreetly moved from the place of death to a refrigerated morgue where they are confined and kept until burial or cremation. We rarely see dead bodies in our daily lives, even though people die everyday. Why are we hiding from the dead? Is it because keeping death tucked away helps to support the illusion that life is infinite? When we have an intimate relationship with death, we also have an intimate relationship with spirit. It's impossible to witness death and not feel the impermanence of the physical form and the infinite nature of the spirit.

Ancestrally, so many of us are deeply removed from the death rituals that are rooted in honouring the earth as our home. Culturally, we don't really know what to do when death occurs. People don't know what to say, how to act, or how to be. When Blue and Ollie died, any call I had to have about their death with a vet or pet-related service was immediately met with an awkward energy and a massive decrease in volume. People's voices get softer and higher pitched, and the topic is danced around. There is a sense of shame, sadness, and regret. We're so removed from our connection to the land that we don't know what to do with a body when it dies, even though we each live in a body that will one day die. Dead bodies seem to just disappear within seconds, and life continues on. We rarely think about what happens to people's bodies, where they go and what is done. We're even scared to touch dead bodies, as if doing so increases our chances of dying.

Our imbalanced relationships with death reflect our malnourished relationships with the dark. We don't really know how to be with either. Befriending death is a journey that calls to some of us, and requires all of us. Death is the most permanent reminder that we are not in control, and that our lives are just as vulnerable as the beings that end up on our dinner plates or seen as less than us. Death asks us to get our hands dirty, to spend time with the earth and to remember that we come from the earth and we will return there. To remember the wisdom that travels in our blood and to resist the temptation to be righteous. Experiencing death means getting dirt in your fingernails and sweat stains on your clothes. It isn't clean and pure, just like grief isn't a pre-packaged emotion that you can have and be done with within a moment's notice. Grief is one of the gifts from death that asks us to open our eyes and hearts to witnessing beauty in places that we would usually miss. Grief asks us to move slower and maybe even allow ourselves to be messy. Death isn't pretty. When Ollie died, the vet put a pee pad beneath his body because when the body dies it releases and surrenders. When Ollie took his last breath, his eyes were partially open, his tongue was sticking out of his mouth and a puddle of excretion soaked around him. As the body dies it begins to smell and those smells are natural, just like the pungent smell in Ollie's mouth was a symptom of his departure. The irony is that witnessing the uncensored truth of life and death is truly beautiful. When a woman gives birth, it is messy, bloody and miraculous. We have tried our best to conceal the truth of life and death by quickly cleaning up a new born baby and swaddling it in a fresh white blanket, or immediately hiding a dead body in a thick black body bag. By doing this, we are treating ourselves as incapable. Once again, we are hiding from the dark and pretending that the light is all there is. By doing this, we are creating and building an unnatural balance, which at some point must rebalance itself. We are removing ourselves from the experience. We are shutting off a natural and necessary connection to the cycle of life. We are pretending that we are only here for an experience and that we can hand select what we want and what we don't want. We are treating life as a game and earth as the game board that we can use and throw out once we are done with it. Life and death work together. To embrace life we must welcome death, in the same way that Ollie joyfully and knowingly welcomed the vet who would later kill him, into his home.

OLLIE AND BLUE

Two of my Greatest Teachers

What comes up for you when you think of death?

What death rituals have you witnessed?

What are your ancestor's death rituals and traditions?

When was the last time you got your hands dirty?

Is there a connection for you between death and the dark?

What are your community's death traditions?

When was the last time you saw a dead body?

What was that experience like?

When was the last time you witnessed a birth?

What was that like?

Do you allow yourself to feel messy?

"May wolf spirit take you on his back
In flight
With all your senses open
So that you experience the rare clarity
Of the mountains
And touch the wild beauty of the wind
Soaring above the Earth
Feel the soft moonlight on your skin
Hear the whispering trees
May night embrace you
And the oceans love you
And may all your days be blessed."

– ANANDA AMANET REID

a message my aunt wrote to me
in my birthday card in 2020

FLYING ARROW

◆

"All the deaths of all living things feed life;
What does our death feed?
All of life's deaths mean that life continues;
What does our death mean?"

- STEPHEN JENKINSON, DIE WISE

We didn't know why we were going, but when Faris posed the possibility of going to India for a few days, I immediately knew that our destination was a place called Varanasi. At the time, I didn't know anything about it, including where it was or what it was known for. When we realised that we had a few days off of work, we had booked our tickets, found a guest house on the Ganges to stay, packed our bags, and boarded a plane. Our arrival was jolting. As soon as our plane landed, a thick blanket of polarising energy enveloped my body, as if I were sitting in a pool of fire and ice. As we drove on the dirt road highways from the airport, we both noticed various trucks that either had cabs on top or were simply filled with people, sitting in a circle in the back. It reminded me of traveling in Jakarta as a kid, where the tops of moving trains were covered with hundreds of people miraculously sitting and standing together as if they were glued to the surface. As more trucks passed us, I began to realise that the people in the back were always gathered around something, placing their hands towards it or on top of a large box or something that was laid down below them. When I asked our cab driver, he responded in a high-pitched, grainy voice as if he was being strangled. It was hard to make out the words except for four unmistakable sounds: bodies, death, dying, and holy. These were human bodies, dead or dying. We later discovered that Varanasi was a sacred part of India, a holy location where people came to die so that their bodies could be cremated at the great burial site on the Ganges river edge. In Hindu culture, having your body burned here is seen as a great honour and privilege. The river itself is also seen as a place of purification, one where people bathe and release their sins. In Varanasi, like many parts of India and Asia, death is unavoidable; it is everywhere. Death isn't hidden in the same way that it is in the West, and it walks the streets with the same freedom that the sacred cows do. We had not yet really understood what we were getting ourselves into, but it was beginning to feel as though we had been invited to Varanasi.

India isn't the place that gradually and gently welcomes you, giving you time and space to adjust to its frequency. You are in it from the moment you set foot on the land and Varanasi is the epitome of this, with no breaks. In Varanasi, everything revolves around the Ganges and the daily rituals that honour life and death. In the mornings, individuals, pilgrims and families gather on the colourful steps of the Ghat to bathe, pray and play together in the river, to start the day and honour the rising sun. Later, as the sun drops below the horizon, the presence of death emerges from the river's dark abyss as the locals prepare for the daily burning rituals. We were told that as many as 200 people are cremated each day here. It wasn't until our last day that we climbed onto one of the creaky wooden river boats at dusk to witness the death ceremony that we apparently had come for. The mysterious water felt both eerie and beautiful. This was the first time I witnessed the harmonious dance of dark and light with my own eyes. Candles decorated the scene, floating above the midnight water and bobbing up and down with the gentle current. Most tourists resisted the urge to bathe, swim, or touch the Ganges as it is known to be exceptionally polluted with bacteria and germs from all kinds of wastes being dumped, including human remains. It was the river of life and death. I even noticed myself feeling worried when I accidentally touched the water as I gently placed a lotus flower offering onto its surface that a sweet local girl had coerced me into buying from her minutes earlier. The dichotomy of experiences that filled the air in Varanasi was both compelling and maddening. I later learned that some people pilgrimage to this place so eager to die here that they jump into the river, committing suicide. Having your body burned in ceremony was a deep privilege and required certain social status and finances that many did not have. Photos capture the glaring images of bodies floating at the surface, providing nourishment for vultures who smell their dead bodies from miles away.

As we sat a few meters from the ghat, we breathed in this sensationally haunting scene: large pyres of wood stacked with bodies wrapped in golden cloth atop, burning in large flames. The pungent smell of melting flesh mixed with the delicate scents of sandalwood and rose, blanketing the air. No where else in the world had I witnessed a celebration of death quite like this. This ancient ceremony pierced my heart like a flying arrow. There was something here that pulled my mind in directions that I didn't know of. Even though in most ways, I felt separate, I also felt a part of me; a wild part of me, awakening. I left with unanswerable questions. Questions that took me to an unknown place that allowed fear to dance hand in hand with curiosity, knowing, and truth. This place was raw and messy, and nothing could ever be hidden here. It reminded me of the stories I had read from the past. It reminded me of the little girl in Tibet who's dead body was placed atop a mountain to be eaten by vultures. It made me think about the word 'savage' and how we use it to describe behaviours that make us uncomfortable. It seemed more savage to deny and hide death, than to be with it. Varanasi felt like duality's playground. It called me the way that the elders, runes, and animals did. It felt like home the way that the wild does. These were the places where I found the parts of myself that were missing, the wisdom, magic, and courage that were revealed by darkness. I was becoming endarkened. These were the places that I felt most connected to my ancestors, because I knew they felt just as welcome here as I did. I knew that this would be a moment in my life that I would always remember and that the memory of it would continue to guide me through all that life and death would bring me.

YR
Remind me
To hold focus
With silent aim
Your taut bow
Skadi
Releases a true flying arrow
You sustain life by taking life
The taste and smell
Of blood
Are your sacraments

- INGRID KINCAID

IT TAKES A VILLAGE

Everything that I've needed has always been living inside of me. I've pulled off a pretty convincing act of being deeply independent since I was a little girl, and the truth is that there are some powerful pillars in my life whom without, this book wouldn't be here and my story would be very different. Life takes you on a continuous journey through duality; fire and ice, creation and destruction. The dark has taught me that every quality of life has an offering. I believe that every being that we cross paths with has something for us: a message, a lesson, a gift, love. I am grateful for every being who has entered my life or walked alongside me whether they were part of a creation or a destruction. Everyone I've encountered made a significant mark on my life map, and I know who I am because of the journeys I have walked with them. You are all scattered throughout this book, whether in the lines or in between them, and I am grateful for you. You have taught me how to stay standing as the wind blows, how to choose and walk impossible paths, and how to tell my hardest truths honestly and with a straight face.

Thank you for knowing me.
Thank you for seeing me.
Thank you for teaching me.
Thank you for loving me.

First, my beloved partner Faris, the best team mate and my favourite person in the world, as well as the Oweis clan.
A special thanks to my family, Mum, Dad, Sam, Tori, and Ananda
To my dogs and fierce guardians in life and death, Ollie, and Blue
To my wise teachers, Lynnette, Divi, and Ingrid
To my friends, sisters, and soulmates who've journeyed with me
And to my amazing book team, Michelle, Paulina, Heather, and Janaa
I love you.

I acknowledge that this book
was created on the unceded traditional territories
belonging to a number of Indigenous peoples
including the Tonkawa, Jumanos, Kickapoo,
Comanche and Apache tribes.
I am grateful to live, work,
and play here in Austin, Texas
on a land that is shared by many.

A NOTE FROM THE AUTHOR

The vision for this book began six years ago on an island in Greece. Gathered there with Cheryl Strayed, her husband and kids, and a group of creatives, I began to write my story. For two weeks, I wrote what happened. When I returned home to Dubai, I realised that I wasn't ready to fully go there. My story was still becoming. So I waited. While I waited, I wrote and hid my writing deep inside the dark crevices of my laptop. One winter, I travelled to our family ranch in Alberta and wrote for two weeks. Those chapters followed the others into the cave. I moved to Austin, Texas, and my book began to speak to me again. This time, it was louder. I started to write again. Slowly, after five years, the book began to reveal itself to me. My story was ready to be told. I do believe we all have a story inside of us. I know you do too. If reading my story has woken up a part of you that has been dormant inside, I encourage you to start expressing it. It will be a journey worth experiencing, and it will begin in the dark.

Love, Chloe

channeledbychloe.com @channeledbychloe

ᛦ YR

The rune that I pulled for you is YR. This is the rune that I end my book with (flip back a few pages to see the poem by Ingrid Kincaid). You are at a pause in life, an intentional pause. As you pull back the bow, you feel the pressure of the pause in your body. A pause requires you to hold the energy in your hands. You feel the heat and tension. Where are you aiming your arrow? Where are you going to direct it? As you pause you know that so much is to come, soon. This is not a time to be afraid. Your arrow will fly further if you stand tall and strong. Keep your feet rooted. Stay focused. You're going somewhere...

Made in the USA
Monee, IL
23 July 2021